The Autonomic Healing of Self ©

"Dr. Ajrawat's Air-Pulse Autonomic Meditation Therapy®"

A Breakthrough Self-Administered Cognitive and Medical Therapy for The New Age

To: Salvatore F. Fiscina, MD

With Compliments

The Autonomic Healing of Self ©

"Dr. Ajrawat's Air-Pulse Autonomic Meditation Therapy®"

A Breakthrough Self-Administered Cognitive and Medical Therapy for The New Age

By Paramjit Singh Ajrawat, M.D.

ISBN: 978-0-615-38541-9

Library of Congress - Copy Right Office - Control Number: 1-88D7VT - Book and Instructional DVD

Note: To protect their privacy, only the first names or initials of patients have been used.

The following terms are copyrighted and/or trademarked: Dr. Ajrawat's Air-Pulse Autonomic Meditation Therapy®, Ajrawat Air-Pulse Autonomic Therapy®, Autonomic Healing™, Ajrawat Air-Pulse Maneuver™, Ajrawat Air-Pulse Homeostatic Reflex™, Autonomic Bliss™, Autonomic Balance™, Autonomic Enlightenment™, Air-Pulse Amygdala Therapy™, Ajrawat Air-Pulse Navel Breathing™, Unitary Consciousness™, Bi-directional Psychosomatic Autonomic Feedback™, Dr. Ajrawat's Air-Pulse Marathon™.

Table of Contents

Disclaimer and Notice

I have written *The Autonomic Healing of Self* and produced the accompanying DVD to educate mankind about my invention, and to help people who suffer from pain and stress. My goal is to help you understand how the human mind and body work, so you can heal your emotional and physical pain. No matter what your problem might be, you must first consult your personal physician and get the necessary help you need before using the methods I describe. *The Autonomic Healing of Self* and accompanying DVD are for educational purposes only. Ajrawat Air-Pulse Autonomic Therapy must be practiced in a safe and quiet environment.

By purchasing this book, you have the right to practice Ajrawat Air-Pulse Autonomic Therapy. In all other cases, it can only be administered by Dr. P.S. Ajrawat, its founder and inventor, or by professionals duly trained, certified, and licensed to administer it, based on their knowledge, medical credentials, and having passed a written exam offered by Dr. Ajrawat's Air-Pulse Autonomic Meditation Therapy Foundation. Dr. Ajrawat's Air-Pulse Autonomic Meditation Therapy is copyrighted, federally registered, and patented.

Affirmation and Oath

Below you will find a Daily Affirmation that you should recite at the start of every day, as well as a Daily Oath for the proper use of Ajrawat Air-Pulse Autonomic Meditation Therapy.

Daily Affirmation

I affirm to myself that I am an individual in my own right, a unitary consciousness as well as part of the greater consciousness manifested through my parents. I further affirm that I am the very best individual mankind has seen, and I believe in the equality of all mankind. I carve my own destiny through knowledge, imagination, creativity, hard work, the practice of correct principles, and awareness of self. During my brief journey through life, I aspire to be happy and keep others happy by being kind, caring, and considerate. I further affirm that I will do good actions and never get deterred by tyranny or oppression of any kind. I must meditate and exercise daily, and eat a balanced diet. I further accept and acknowledge the truth that one can take no possessions from this world, so I will use all efforts to enjoy myself, my family, and friends without getting overly attached or becoming judgmental. I must say my daily prayers, be in touch with my creator, and give my thanks for making me the blessing I am.

Daily Oath

I solemnly swear that I will use Dr. Ajrawat's Air-Pulse Autonomic Meditation Therapy to make myself mentally and physically healthy and self empowered. I shall practice it for my own personal use, and for the mental and physical benefits I receive from practicing this scientific, non-denominational autonomic meditation therapy. I will use it to help and enhance others, and never to mentally control or put others down. I will not exploit it or use it for monetary benefits. So help me GOD.

Introduction

A New Paradigm for Healing Pain and Stress, and Promoting Lasting Health

More than ever before, all of mankind is searching for new and effective ways to heal the trauma of emotional and physical pain. Millions suffer from stress, anxiety, depression, and a host of other psychological and emotional problems, yet mainstream modern medicine has too often failed to provide healthy and effective pain relief. Many of the cures offered by traditional medicine do more harm than good. Illnesses are misdiagnosed, improper medications are prescribed, and the pain sufferer gets caught in a vicious cycle of unsuccessful remedies because, for the most part, traditional approaches fail to understand that body and mind are interrelated entities that must be treated together to ensure human health.

As a qualified pain specialist over the last 25 years, I have developed a holistic and highly effective meditation therapy that has helped hundreds of my patients overcome stress, anxiety, depression, and a host of other emotional ailments. *The Autonomic Healing of Self* describes a revolutionary new way of treating pain. Its centerpiece is Ajrawat Air-Pulse Autonomic Therapy, the world's first scientifically based meditation therapy, which activates the natural healing powers of the body's autonomic nervous system to restore balance in both body and mind. Ajrawat Air-Pulse Autonomic Therapy is natural, requires no religious beliefs or rituals, and can be self-administered by anyone, at any time or place. Based on scientific principles and research, it does not cater to any religious philosophy. It involves meditation on one's self and body, without involving any mantras, rituals, or distractions. It is non-intrusive, preserves the autonomy of the individual, and is free of any cost.

Combining a spiritual and scientific approach in meditation for the first time, Ajrawat Air-Pulse Autonomic Therapy is solidly based on general systems theory—the understanding that various biochemical structures in our bodies, such as hormones, neurotransmitters, and noxious stimuli, can determine the quality of a person's mental or physical health. Based on my concept of Bidirectional Psychosomatic Autonomic Feedback, Ajrawat Air-Pulse Autonomic Therapy enables individuals to consciously control, regulate, and restore these biochemical structures, and thereby attain and maintain optimum health. It dispels the long-held belief that involuntary processes of the human mind and body cannot be manipulated at will to restore one's health.

For almost 15 years, I have used Ajrawat Air-Pulse Autonomic Therapy to successfully treat a wide range of chronic conditions. Many patients come to me suffering from serious physical illnesses and injuries, such as back and neck pain, diabetes, and severe headaches. I use Autonomic Therapy as part of a comprehensive pain treatment program to help these patients.

But Ajrawat Air-Pulse Autonomic Therapy (also called Khalistani Meditation Therapy) can also be used, alone and without supervision, by healthy people, and well as those suffering from any kind of emotional or physical ailment. It can be used to treat common emotional problems, such as anxiety, stress, and depression, from a scientifically proven perspective. It can be employed as a part of a one's daily routine, starting in high school or college, as a preventive measure against stress, anxiety, depression, negative peer pressure, substance abuse, and cigarette smoking, and to build self-esteem, self-confidence, insightfulness, and one's personal identity. As a medical therapy, Ajrawat Air-Pulse Autonomic Therapy can be used to treat practically every psychological, psychiatric, and medical illness.

Until now, it has been believed that psychological or psychiatric illnesses were primarily the result of one's environment, psychological makeup, and genetic disposition. Hence psychoanalysis, psychotherapy, and medication were considered the major ways of treating these disorders.

But now, with better research and technology, a fundamental shift is taking place. We have learned that brain chemistry has a profound impact on our thoughts, emotions, and behavior. For example, individuals who abuse drugs like alcohol, cocaine, marijuana, or even narcotic analgesics, can develop permanent damage to the brain resulting from decreased circulation and perfusion of the cortex, temporal lobes, and other parts of the brain. Changes in neurobiology can lead to cognitive, emotional, behavioral, and mood changes, and eventually to the development of specific emotional and psychological disorders.

Many of the common problems people encounter in life, such as stress, anxiety, and depression, as well as marital problems, drug addiction, and domestic violence, are invariably related to pathologic changes in brain neurobiology and neurochemistry. With this knowledge, we now have the power to correct the brain's chemistry and lead more integrated, healthy lives.

Ajrawat Air-Pulse Autonomic Therapy presents an entirely new paradigm for understanding human thought processes, emotions, behavior, spirituality, and religion. By restoring balance to mind and body, it can help people moderate their stress, anger, depression, and oppositional behavior, while gaining self-esteem and self-confidence in the process. It can help physicians, lawyers, politicians, businessmen, law enforcement officials, intelligence personnel, teachers, clergy, and others who work in high stress occupations. School children can use the therapy to deal with problems like bullies and peer pressure. College students can use it to lessen stress. Women can use it to deal with problems at home or in the workplace. It can help individuals who are using drugs, involved in violence, and serving jail time. In short, everyone can achieve a better emotional and physical state by using Ajrawat Air-Pulse Autonomic Therapy. By practicing it on a regular basis in combination with Ajrawat Air-Pulse Maneuver and by activating Ajrawat Air-Pulse Homeostatic Reflex, one can achieve Autonomic Bliss, Autonomic Balance, and Autonomic Enlightenment.

The proof is in the testimonies of hundreds of my patients. B.F. is one such example.

"I am a living proof that Dr. Ajrawat's treatments not only work but actually transform you," he says. "I came to see him with pain in my left elbow and right shoulder. I have received trigger point injections, medication, and physical therapy but that is only one piece of the puzzle.

"The main thing I received was the gift of Dr. Ajrawat's meditation therapy. This meditation takes only a few minutes a day, and the relaxation and wellness you feel counteracts a lot of pain by itself. When you're not thinking about pain, you don't walk around upset and upsetting others. And to top it off, I've lost thirty pounds due to this technique in less than two months. Something this simple has definitely changed my life."

Mr. Akram is yet another example.

"I was terribly injured in a car accident about two years ago," he says. "My knee and two toes were broken as a result of the accident, leaving my entire leg in a very critical condition. I was treated by highly qualified and competent doctors, but their prolonged treatment was ineffective and caused further complications. Even after two surgeries were performed, I still couldn't stand or walk. Also, the pain in my leg was so awful that it kept me awake many nights. I didn't think I was ever going to walk again.

"In a desperate time like this, when my family and I had lost all hope, I was lucky to come across Dr. Ajrawat. I was very hesitant due to my previous experience, but I started treatment again at his Washington Pain Management Center. Under Dr. Ajrawat's supervision and care for only two weeks, I saw and felt positive changes that I hadn't experienced over the past year. The pain disappeared entirely, and I am now able to walk properly. With his superior medical practice and innovative pain management procedures, Dr. Ajrawat achieved what had seemed impossible. Air-Pulse Autonomic Meditation Therapy has played a vital part in my recovery."

The Autonomic Healing of Self is a book of practical solutions to the complex problem of pain. Chapter One examines how I treated several patients, to give an overview of the Bio-Psychosocial Model of pain management, a holistic treatment approach that views mind and body as inseparable, interrelated parts of the human being. I then describe how Ajrawat Air-Pulse Autonomic Therapy offers a new paradigm for healing emotional and physical pain. As a scientifically based meditation, it goes beyond traditional, non-scientific meditation by activating the restorative powers of the parasympathetic nervous system, to re-establish lost homeostasis in the body's systems.

Chapter Two describes my personal journey as a pain management specialist. I look at how a childhood injury gave me insight into the nature of pain and life-long sympathy for those who suffer from its chronic effects. I describe my path to the Bio-Psychosocial Model, and look at how emotional pain, brain-based in nature, is originated and perpetuated on a personal, family, and societal level, with profound consequences for all of mankind. I then look at how brain-based science and Ajrawat Air-Pulse Autonomic Therapy offer a new paradigm for healing our individual and cultural ills.

Chapter Three looks closely at how the nervous system, the endocrine system, and the human brain function, and how the body responds to stress. I then look in detail at how scientifically based Ajrawat Air-Pulse Autonomic Therapy restores and heals the systems of the body, and how it can be practiced by anyone, at any time, to restore and maintain emotional and physical health.

Chapter Four describes how I use a dynamic, multi-modality approach to treat chronic physical pain. I look at how pain is experienced by the body and at the challenges posed by chronic pain. I explain the eight core therapeutic practices that guide my practice, and the multi-modality treatments that I use, in addition to Ajrawat Air-Pulse Autonomic Therapy, to treat chronic physical pain. Then, by examining case histories of my patients, I show how these treatments have made a profound difference in the lives of real people.

Chapter Five discusses in detail over two dozen emotional, psychiatric, and physical disorders and how I treat them, again using case histories from my practice. I define each disorder, explain its symptoms, causes, and risk factors, and show how I evaluate, diagnose, and treat it.

Chapter Six examines how we can achieve true peace, balance, and spirituality through regular use of Ajrawat Air-Pulse Autonomic Therapy. While not discounting the beauty or utility of the world's religions—for I am a religious man myself—I describe how we must move beyond the blind conditioning of dogma, whether religious, political, or social in nature, to achieve a higher spiritual consciousness through scientific means.

Finally, Chapter Seven describes a comprehensive program you can follow at home to regain and maintain your emotional and physical health. I discuss how diet, daily exercise and meditation, and a proper approach to work, creativity, and relaxation, can become a life-long path to freedom from pain in all its forms.

Though I have addressed a wide range of emotional and physical illnesses that can be alleviated or healed by Ajrawat Air-Pulse Autonomic Therapy, it is beyond the scope of this book to cover in detail every psychiatric and physical disorder or condition that could be helped by this therapy. In addition, the treatments described in this book should not substitute for treatment by your personal physician. You should consult your personal physician before trying any of the methods I describe. Nevertheless, because it is a natural, non-invasive, and self-administered therapy, Ajrawat Air-Pulse Autonomic Therapy has no harmful side effects. Whatever your particular health issues, you should make it a routine part of your life to gain the many benefits of mental and physical health. I also welcome any interested parties to conduct research or studies of its various therapeutic effects. Those interested in doing so should contact Dr. Ajrawat's Air-Pulse Autonomic Meditation Therapy Foundation at the address listed in the appendix.

In the end, *The Autonomic Healing of Self* is a book of practical solutions. I hope you will use Ajrawat Air-Pulse Autonomic Therapy to heal the stress, anxiety, and depression in your life. If you suffer from more serious illnesses or conditions, it can become part of a multi-modality treatment plan. In either case, there is now a scientific way to heal the body's emotional and physical disorders, which I believe has extraordinary implications for all of mankind.

Paramjit Singh Ajrawat, M.D.
Washington, D.C.
Dec. 1, 2010

Chapter 1

Ajrawat Air-Pulse Autonomic Therapy:
A Scientific Breakthrough in
Healing Emotional Pain and Stress

On a recent New Year's Day, while visiting her family in Michigan, Kate was walking down the stairs in socks, both hands full of Christmas presents. Her feet slipped out from under her and she bounced on her bottom all the way down the stairway.

At first she was merely glad that no one was home to witness her embarrassment. However, as she regained her feet, she noticed her whole body was in pain.

"It felt like I had just been beaten up or something," Kate recalled. "I blew it off. Of course I would be sore—I just fell down half a flight of stairs."

Kate had to get home to Maryland. She was a nursing student and school was starting up again soon. She loaded her car and drove from Michigan to Maryland, a nine-hour trip. The entire time she was switching positions because her back hurt terribly and she could not get comfortable. She had fallen on a Friday and by Sunday friends noticed she was in great pain and limping slightly. One friend suggested she go to the doctor to get it checked out.

That Monday she couldn't see her primary care provider, so she went to an urgent care center. After the exam, they took x-rays of Kate's lower back and hips. She had fractured her coccyx or tailbone. The urgent care physician prescribed pain medication and referred her to an orthopedist for follow up.

Later that week Kate met with the orthopedist. He explained that this type of fracture could not be fixated (put in a cast), so it would take longer to heal.

"I asked him how long it would take, and he replied up to three or four months," Kate remembered. "I asked him what I would do in the meantime. He refilled my pain medication prescription, but suggested that I use the medication sparingly and slowly try to wean myself off it. What he didn't realize was that the medication was the only thing keeping me from crying out in pain. Some of the maneuvers he made me do during the exam were very painful, even though I was fully medicated."

The orthopedist recommended that Kate try to do as little as possible and rest. If she continued to have problems, he suggested she follow up with her primary care provider. He gave Kate her x-ray and prescription and sent her on her way.

"What a waste of time. I told him I was starting nursing school in two weeks. How was I supposed to do minimal activity with lectures and clinical work starting? Plus, he didn't even ask if I had roommates or family to help me if I was going to be resting so much. I live alone with my two dogs. Who was going to walk them? Who was going to make dinner and do the laundry if I was sequestered on the couch, unable to move?"

Nevertheless, Kate tried a week of minimal activity and took her pain medication as scheduled. It was not an easy week. Every time she changed positions or stood up from a seated position, she felt the worst pain of her life. The pain medicine mitigated some of the agony, but Kate found no true relief. She went back to the urgent care doctor whom she had seen for her first visit. Kate asked her if there was anything else that could be done. Very reluctantly, the urgent care doctor prescribed a stronger pain medication, but warned Kate that she shouldn't get used to it.

"I asked the doctor what I was supposed to do about school and daily living," Kate told me. "She basically said just deal with it and gave me my prescription. I was livid. The orthopedist had said this could take three to four months to heal and that I could have residual pain for up to a year. And she gives me two weeks worth of new medication and tells me to deal with it? I thought, 'There has to be something better than this.'"

Later that evening, Kate researched pain management centers for the Washington D.C. area and found my website. She called and made an appointment the following day.

During our first sessions together, I treated Kate with nerve blocks and appropriate pharmacological remedies, as well as with Ajrawat Air-Pulse Autonomic Therapy, part of the multi-modality treatments I use with chronic pain patients. In addition, I sat down with her and explained my theories about pain and how it should be treated.

"I learned that pain is much more than just physical," Kate remembered. "It can be mental, emotional, or spiritual. I learned that these aspects of pain, if not also resolved and treated, can be barriers to treating any current illness or injury at hand."

Kate was suffering not only from her persistent back injury and incapacitation, but also from great emotional and psychological pain, not only related to her injury but to issues that went far deeper than her body. As I treated her back, I also helped Kate deal with that psychological and emotional trauma, to help her heal spiritually as well as physically.

"Dr. Ajrawat helped me explore my past experiences, all the way back to childhood, to help determine what could be exacerbating the deep depression I had carried with me for so many years. Through his autonomic therapy, he helped me regain confidence in myself, to believe that I could get better not just physically but mentally as well. During meditation I focused on positive affirmations and reflected on my long-term goals: to lose physical weight, but also to release the mental weight I had been carrying around for so long.

"Over the course of several weeks," Kate said, "as my back pain became more tolerable, I noticed my attitude changing. I wasn't overburdened by the anxieties that had plagued me in the past. I was sleeping better and waking up at the time I should have been all along. As I sat there self-relaxing during meditation, I thought positively and refused to dwell on the pain of the past. After I finished each meditation, I felt like I was becoming a new person. Each day was a new day to be thankful for. The past was the past and I couldn't let that bother me now.

"It was amazing for me to realize how intertwined the emotional and physical symptoms of pain can be, and how you cannot treat one without the other. Dr. Ajrawat's holistic approach to pain management was unlike any type of treatment for any illness I had ever encountered. His approach enabled me to break the cycle of mental pain I had been living with for so long, and to heal my chronic back pain successfully."

Like Kate, Sandra could not heal physically until she also healed emotionally. After her son was murdered in 1997, Sandra suffered from severe depression.

"The horrific part of my son's demise was that the crime was committed by one of his friends," she told me. "I was treated for depression in numerous hospitals after his death. For the past 13 years I had been seeing a psychiatrist monthly. Still, my son's death continued to anger and haunt me."

Sandra's situation wasn't helped when she began experiencing severe and chronic physical pain in her mid-40s, which lasted for the next eight years.

"Unfortunately, that was the beginning of an eight-year nightmare. During that time I saw one doctor after another, even some in foreign counties. Some doctors suggested that it was all in my mind. I was finally diagnosed with pelvic pain, but after running several tests they couldn't find anything. No one could find what was causing the pain."

In 2004 a doctor detected cysts in Sandra's pelvic area and said the pain would go away if they were removed. She had the operation, but the pain remained. She continued to see doctor after doctor over the next few years. Then a doctor detected that Sandra had fibroids as large as oranges and insisted this was her problem. She had a hysterectomy, but once again the pain didn't go away.

Frustrated and disgusted, Sandra went to the renowned Johns Hopkins University Hospital, where doctors ran more tests and found nothing. Johns Hopkins then referred her to a pain specialist. Sandra saw her twice weekly, but she did nothing to solve Sandra's problems.

Sandra became aware of my services in June 2010 and contacted me. After a detailed physical examination and evaluation of her health history, I was able to diagnose her problem. She was suffering from myofascial pain confined to her lower back, pelvic area, and right upper and inner thigh area, which was causing her both local and referred pain. In addition, Sandra had a skeletal disproportion—that is, her short leg perpetuated her pelvic pain. Her anxiety, depression, and anger regarding her son's death complemented the intensity of her physical pain, and her physical pain in turn fueled her anxiety and depression. This non-stop pain and stress cycle was finally broken by correct diagnosis and hands-on intervention, including nerve blocks, trigger point injections, physical therapy, strengthening and stretching exercises, pain medication, and, most importantly for her mental anguish, anxiety, and depression, Ajrawat Air-Pulse Autonomic Therapy.

After a month of multimodality treatments, Sandra's pain decreased significantly, by almost 80%. Her mood and outlook were transformed. She felt happy and in control. She began to enjoy her life without feeling stuck and angry.

"Not only has Dr. Ajrawat helped me with my physical pain," she says today, "he has also freed me from years of spiritual and emotional bondage. For years I searched in vain for relief. Even Johns Hopkins Hospital, one of the greatest in the world, could not help me. Now I feel vibrant and alive again. Through his Air-Pulse Autonomic Meditation Therapy, my soul has been spiritually cleansed from the pain, hate, and anger I've carried for the last 13 years. I've even forgiven the person who killed my son. Not for him, but for me. My mind is free now, and I can go on with my life. For the first time in a long time, I'm living again. I have the power and the will to live and love life. I can finally celebrate past memories of my son and feel good. Where there is no peace, there is no power. I've learned that when you complain, you remain. I've decided to praise and be raised. Dr. Ajrawat's dedication, devotion, and expertise have erased years of grief and sorrow from my life."

The Bio-Psychosocial Model:
Treating Mind and Body as One

Physical and emotional suffering have plagued mankind since the beginning of time. Today, many thousands of Americans become disabled because of pain and stress, resulting in millions of lost work hours annually and billions of dollars spent on medical treatments.

Traditional models of pain relief fail because they are not based on the latest scientific evidence. To this day, most physicians still favor the biomedical model (also known as the dualistic model) to understand and treat pain. (Dualism is the belief that the world is composed of distinct and mutually exclusive parts.) The biomedical model treats the body and the mind as two separate entities that are opposed to each other. It tends to ignore the psychosocial components—the patient's mental state, family, work, and social environment. This was the problem faced by Kate and Sandra, and hundreds of other patients I have seen.

When a patient experiences pain, the biomedical model has trained the physician to believe that the cause is either solely in the body or solely in the mind, but not in both. Looking at those two options, the physician's tendency is to rule out one against the other rather than consider both. The prejudice in this model is that the causes of most pain are located in the body, and so the doctor focuses only on the body as the source of the ailment.

Of course, the body can be the source of pain, but bodily causes are often misdiagnosed, while the patient's emotional state and social milieu are ignored altogether.

One example would be a person working in a stressful environment who develops headaches, arthritis, and perhaps ulcers as well. The social environment leads to a physical symptom, and the resulting pain cannot be treated apart from its environmental causes. Another example would be the person injured in an automobile accident who suffers chronic pain and as a result descends into clinical depression. That depression, in turn, will affect every aspect of the person's life and will worsen the physical pain he or she suffers. If the depression is not treated in conjunction with the injury, the patient will make little progress.

As a qualified, experienced, and conservative pain specialist, I believe most pain and stress could be remedied with much less physical, emotional, and financial cost, but only if the medical community adopts a new frame of reference to evaluate and treat pain. As shown by the stories of Kate and Sandra, the prevalent frame of reference is faulty and obsolete. Mind and body are not separate entities, but rather intimately connected. Pain is not a uni-dimensional problem rooted in either physical or psychological causes. I have treated hundreds of pain patients who were told by their treating physicians that their pain was imaginary and that they needed to consult psychiatrists because their x-rays, scans, and labs were negative. Yet, I can assure you, their pain was all too real. And it was also treatable.

The misguided biomedical model has left millions of pain sufferers feeling disenfranchised, angry, and frustrated. Drug dependence or addiction, as well as lingering physical disability, are often the result. Intimate relationships are lost, families fall apart, and jobs and gainful employment disappear. All too often, children of chronic pain sufferers develop their own disability syndromes, the result of living with disabled parents.

Adding to this problem is a severe shortage of trained and certified pain specialists. Too many doctors specializing in pain treatment lack proper credentials or are simply self-proclaimed "experts." This only increases the frustration and anger of pain patients desperately seeking appropriate help.

Following the cardinal rule "Do No Harm," I have become a tireless advocate for conservative, effective, and multi-dimensional pain treatment. My practice is based on the Bio-Psychosocial Model of illness, which is founded on general systems theory, established by pioneers in the fields of pain medicine and pain management. According to this model, every system is organized into multiple levels, and each level of a system communicates with and is affected by those levels above and below it.

Take the human body as an example of how systems theory works. Its complex organization consists of many levels, starting with subcellular structures and rising through the nerves, tissues, organs, and other parts of the body. The levels of the body also include the person's mind and emotions, as well as the individual's entire social setting, including his or her environment, family, work, society, culture, and environment.

Understood in this way, the body cannot be separated from mind nor can mind and body be separated from their environment. The family affects the mind and emotions; trauma to the body affects the person's work environment; depression affects the person's social life, and so on. Each of these levels communicates with all other levels through bidirectional feedback. A disturbance at any of these levels, whether from physical trauma, psychological trauma, or changes in the environment, will in turn affect all other levels and call various defense mechanisms into play. When any of these defense mechanisms fail, the result is both physical and emotional illness.

Ajrawat Air-Pulse Autonomic Therapy: A New Paradigm for Treating Emotional Pain

I used many medical approaches in combination to treat Kate and Sandra successfully, and one of the most important techniques that helped them was Ajrawat Air-Pulse Autonomic Therapy, a natural, scientific, and cognitive medical therapy I invented in 1996. Over many years of use with patients, I have found this therapy to be a highly effective tool for treating physical and emotional pain. I consider it to be a revolutionary advance, capable of healing the division between body and mind, between conscious and unconscious bodily processes, in a way that promotes true recovery and healing from stress, anxiety, and depression, as well as from a wide range of emotional and physical ailments. Ajrawat Air-Pulse Autonomic Therapy is likely to transform not only our approaches to treating pain and stress, but also our basic concepts of spirituality and faith.

It is called Air-Pulse Autonomic Therapy because it employs the natural powers of three basic and vital human functions—breathing (the respiratory system), the pulse (cardiovascular system), and touch—to activate the healing and restorative powers of the autonomic nervous system. It is also cognitive in nature because in addition to healing and balancing the natural systems of the body, it also works to improve the thought processes, or cognitive functioning, of the human mind. Ajrawat Air-Pulse Autonomic Therapy helps people uncover and heal distorted thoughts and perceptions that may be causing them prolonged psychological distress. I have seen patients who were stressed and depressed recover their mental clarity and well being by practicing my autonomic therapy. In contrast to traditional cognitive therapy, Ajrawat Air-Pulse Autonomic Therapy accomplishes these goals through scientifically based biological processes.

Unlike traditional religious meditation, Ajrawat Air-Pulse Autonomic Therapy allows individuals to balance body and mind without experiencing the constraints, burdens, or the loss of identity that often accompany ancient meditative practices. It is non-denominational and open to all, regardless of their religious beliefs. In addition, it is based on scientific fact, not belief, rituals, or fantasy. Combining a spiritual and scientific approach in meditation for the first time, it is solidly based on general systems theory—the understanding that various biochemical structures in our bodies, such as hormones, neurotransmitters, and noxious stimuli, can determine the quality of a person's mental or physical health. Ajrawat Air-Pulse Autonomic Therapy enables individuals to consciously control, regulate, and restore these biochemical structures, thereby activating the natural systems of the body to attain and maintain optimum health. Finally, as stated before, it helps people regulate and improve their cognitive functioning, to feel more focused, aware, and engaged in their daily lives.

For almost 15 years, I have used Air-Pulse Autonomic Therapy to successfully treat a wide range of chronic conditions. Many patients come to me suffering from serious physical illnesses and injuries, such as back and neck pain, diabetes, and severe headaches. I use Air-Pulse Autonomic Therapy as part of a comprehensive pain treatment program to help these patients.

But Ajrawat Air-Pulse Autonomic Therapy can also be used, alone and without supervision, to treat common emotional problems, such as anxiety, stress, and depression, from a scientifically proven perspective. It can be used as a part of a one's daily routine, starting in high school or college, to establish a preventive or prophylactic measure against stress, anxiety, depression, negative peer pressure, and substance abuse, and to build self-esteem, self-confidence, insightfulness, and one's personal identity.

In short, Ajrawat Air-Pulse Autonomic Therapy is a new, self-administered medical therapy that can be used by any individual, healthy or unhealthy, to improve or strengthen his mental and physical health. The ultimate goal of this scientific meditation is to assist individuals in achieving sound mental and physical health by helping them become aware, vibrant, and self-empowered.

A Scientific Meditation to Restore Lost Homeostasis

When the scientific revelation of autonomic therapy came to me in 1994, I did not fully understand the true scope of its therapeutic value. At first I experimented with it, using it as an adjunctive treatment in healing my patients, that is, as one treatment in a range of treatments. But since that time I have become convinced that my invention holds great promise not only as an adjunctive treatment for pain and stress, but as a primary and therefore revolutionary treatment for healing a great range of psychological and physical disorders.

Ajrawat Air-Pulse Autonomic Therapy is based on the understanding that mind and body form one functional unit, with balance between them essential for homeostasis (equilibrium and stability among the body's various systems). In developing and using Autonomic Therapy, I have drawn on my knowledge of human anatomy, physiology, biochemistry, neural mechanisms, pain pathways, nerve endings, neurotransmitters, hormones, neuro-endocrinology, and many other aspects of the mind and body.

The human body's physiological functioning is largely maintained by the autonomic nervous system (ANS). Health and vitality generally result from balance and harmony between the sympathetic and parasympathetic nervous systems, two components of the autonomic nervous system. Air-Pulse Autonomic Therapy is based on my concept of Bi-directional Psychosomatic Autonomic Feedback, which is designed to restore balance to the ANS and improve levels of hormones and neurotransmitters, sympathetic and parasympathetic functions, and general circulation in the body. It utilizes and brings into equilibrium the central nervous system, the cardiac and respiratory systems, and the individual's sense of touch and smile.

The latest research teaches us that emotional and psychological disorders are often the result of structural changes in the brain, such as in levels of neurotransmitters or in blood circulation. Physical and psychological trauma can lead to hypo or hyperactivity in certain areas of the brain, such as the prefrontal cortex, cingulate gyrus, limbic system, left temporal lobe, hippocampus, hypothalamus, basal ganglia, amygdala, and others, which in turn directly affect behavior and mood. Any individual can develop such "negative circuitry," which can continue to be perpetuated by encephalization, or the process of being stored in memory.

Ajrawat Air-Pulse Autonomic Therapy is effective in treating emotional and physical pain because a majority of our emotional and psychological ailments involve an imbalance in the autonomic nervous system. Air-Pulse Autonomic Therapy literally washes away flawed circuitry, while establishing new circuits and links in the memory cycle. In short, Ajrawat Air-Pulse Autonomic Therapy cleanses mind and body from old and negative conditioning, making the mind and body feel fresh and rejuvenated.

My concept is based on my personal belief and a fundamental scientific truth: if you correct the physiology, the psychopathology will automatically be corrected. The results seen in my patients are ample proof of that fact. Over the last 15 years, Ajrawat Air-Pulse Autonomic Therapy has helped thousands of people recover from stress, anxiety, panic attacks, depression, and other forms of emotional pain, as well as a wide range of physical ailments.

The benefits of Ajrawat Air-Pulse Autonomic Therapy are many.

First, there are profound improvements in the physical state of the body. Air-Pulse Autonomic Therapy lowers heart and respiratory rates and blood pressure, improves circulation, and helps people lose weight and boost their energy levels.

In addition, there are profound emotional benefits. Air-Pulse Autonomic Therapy helps individuals quiet mental chatter and live in the present, de-condition their minds against past negative feelings or influences, overcome the barriers and limitations of ego, improve insight, and develop clarity of thought and vision. As the patient becomes more aware and insightful, he or she is able to look inward for solutions. Through persistence, Air-Pulse Autonomic Therapy can lead to the ability to control and optimize emotions, urges, instincts, and behaviors, leading to an evolved state of mind. The individual achieves a balance called Autonomic Balance, a relaxed state of mind and body called Autonomic Bliss, and an awareness of self called Autonomic Enlightenment.

By being nondenominational and open to everyone, persons of any faith can participate without feeling intruded upon, violated, or that they have to follow a rigid set of beliefs or practices. It can be done any time of the day, in any relaxed posture, and without any autosuggestion. The practice of daily Air-Pulse Autonomic Therapy, in combination with walking and jogging, strengthening and stretching exercises, good nutrition, correction of skeletal disproportion, and ergonomics, can help the mind and body acquire and retain their necessary agility, which are essential to good health. Such results can be achieved in a very short time, whereas in other types of meditation it takes forever.

Ajrawat Air-Pulse Autonomic Therapy offers an alternative to traditional treatment methods, such as psychotherapy and medication, which often fail to heal many people's common emotional ills. It can help people who suffer from anger, erratic behavior, or emotional and violent outbursts. It can help people who get stuck on certain thoughts and or have difficulty changing or shifting gears to different, more positive thought patterns. It can help people with low self-esteem and low self-confidence. It can help people who were forced into negative lifestyles, such as prostitution, or who committed crimes in altered states of mind. People suffering from these kinds of problems can self-administer the therapy at any time or place, with scientifically proven results.

At the same time, Ajrawat Air-Pulse Autonomic Therapy can be used in combination with more traditional treatment methods, such psychotherapy and medication, to address more serious and complicated emotional and psychological problems, such as post traumatic stress disorder (PTSD), attention deficit disorder (ADD), obsessive-compulsive disorder (OCD), schizophrenia, and others

The Limitations of Traditional, Non-Scientific Meditation

Before I explain in greater detail how I discovered Ajrawat Air-Pulse Autonomic Therapy and how it works, I want to spend a little time explaining how it is both similar to and different from traditional meditation. Many myths and mysteries surround meditation, and it is necessary to dispel them before going further.

At the dawn of the new millennium, all of humanity is seeking new ways of achieving and maintaining optimum health. No one doubts that advances in medical technology have been phenomenal, yet the efficacy of many of these techniques has come under greater scrutiny. People want to experience positive therapeutic and medical outcomes, while suffering the least amount of iatrogenic morbidity (harmful symptoms or disabilities created in the patient by well-meaning medical interventions). This desire is forcing the entire medical community to concentrate its research and innovation on developing novel methods of treatment, that lead to the greatest benefits with the least amount of harm.

Alternative or integrated medicine has become one of the key approaches for reaching that goal. New techniques and methods are gaining public acceptance, as the limitations of mainstream medicine and traditional approaches have become apparent over time. In fact, major institutions like the National Institute of Health have started entirely new programs to meet this challenge.

While traditional medicine is being challenged by new and alternative approaches, the realms of religion and philosophy are being challenged as well. The present generation is looking for concrete, scientific explanations for ancient meditation traditions and other spiritual practices. Therefore, we are at an important moment in history, when both traditional medicine and traditional religion are being challenged.

While modern science has brought many benefits to the modern world and has helped people with untold numbers of physical ailments, it has failed to provide people with relaxed and functional states of mind. Modern science has helped heal the body, but not the emotions or soul. In contrast, traditional meditation has been used as a spiritual discipline for millennia, and many practitioners believe it to be the ultimate way to relax and merge with universal consciousness. People are increasingly turning to these old and ancient methods to treat pain and stress and achieve peaceful states of mind, since traditional methods of treatment have proven ineffective in providing that relief.

But just as modern science hasn't healed the mind, ancient meditation has failed to heal the body. While meditation has led to positive emotional changes for untold numbers of practitioners, it has failed to address the psycho-biological phenomena that the human mind and body experience at every moment of existence. For example, a certain mantra or posture is not sufficient to help the body regain its lost homeostasis or heal illness. (A mantra is a sound, word, or group of words recited during meditation to achieve spiritual transcendence.)

I must point out that, in my view, if such recitations occur during meditation, then it is no longer true meditation. Instead, it becomes auto-hypnosis, with the end result being a state of trance, which contradicts the ultimate goal of producing a relaxed, focused, and aware mental and physical state, with both mind and body homeostatically and scientifically balanced. The imaginary images, mantras, and chakras conceived by religious philosophy as the prime sources of relaxation have failed to support the balanced functioning of the body. Instead, they only create more intrusion and confusion for individuals who are aspiring to become physically healthy and mentally liberated and free.

Far too often, people who begin a meditation practice to deal with mental and physical ailments often feel dissatisfied, or at times even violated or helpless. They can find themselves trapped by a philosophy or method that seems to take away their autonomy and sense of identity. Despite the widespread use of various meditation techniques, people continue to feel stress in their lives. Hence, a journey meant to bring about the realization of self and physical and mental health instead creates more self-alienation, dependency, and pain.

Until now, no one has created a scientific meditation with proven, therapeutic effects, which utilizes the natural powers of the body to heal both body and mind. Ajrawat Air-Pulse Autonomic Therapy is the first such therapy to offer not only that promise, but proven results in reaching that goal.

My Great Breakthrough: Discovering Ajrawat
Air-Pulse Autonomic Therapy

Because on my understanding of human anatomy, physiology, the nervous system, and how pain is received and processed by the body, a new conception started formulating in my mind in the early 1990s. It dawned upon me that pain and stress sufferers needed a scientifically based meditation or self-administered medical therapy, which, in addition to other treatment modalities, could help them manage and overcome their pain.

Having trained as an anesthesiologist before receiving my fellowship training in pain management, I always knew that a few deep breaths prior to the induction of general anesthesia could instantly relax an apprehensive or very tense patient. I started meditating, focusing on taking deep breaths. But then I discovered something new to add to the meditation, which made it entirely different from traditional types of meditation and that would turn out to have profound implications for my practice.

In addition to closing my eyes and breathing deeply through my nose, I also placed my right thumb on my left wrist's radial pulse. That simple touch distinguishes Ajrawat Air-Pulse Autonomic Therapy from other forms of meditation, for, as I will explain in greater detail in later chapters, it activates the healing power of the parasympathetic nervous system in ways that traditional meditation does not. Instead of just focusing on mind, Ajrawat Air-Pulse Autonomic Therapy activates the physical process of the body to restore lost homeostasis.

By staying focused on my pulse and counting my breaths on each exhalation, I was able to instantly relax myself and bring my heart rate down as well. My pain and stress began to ease, for the first time in many years. I found myself less tense, and much more relaxed, evolved, and insightful.

Eventually I became convinced that this unique technique activated the peripheral nervous system—the sensory and motor nerves extending throughout the body—which in turn activated the central nervous mechanisms and involuntary processes of the body, causing the heart rate and blood pressure to change and the blood vessels to dilate at will, although in a limited and safe way. These changes can in turn contribute to instant relaxation and other positive responses.

My theoretical and practical knowledge of pain and the nervous and respiratory systems had steered me toward a very simple yet amazing scientific discovery. Ajrawat Air-Pulse Autonomic Therapy takes place at the intersection between the psychological and physical manifestations of the body, healing the gap between body and mind. I believe that when the gap between mind and body is eliminated, a new understanding of pain, and of human health in general, will come to pass. It was a scientific revelation for me that Air-Pulse Autonomic Therapy bridges that gap.

I started administering Air-Pulse Autonomic Therapy to pain and stress patients, who also started demonstrating similar therapeutic effects. I started monitoring my patients' pulses and blood pressure, which often dropped significantly every time they engaged in this new technique. Patients reported feeling more relaxed, focused, and energetic after each meditation session.

To understand how Ajrawat Air-Pulse Autonomic Therapy works, realize that neurons carry nerve impulses in different directions in the body, a biological fact that plays a key role in how I treat pain. Sensory neurons are *afferent* neurons, which relay nerve impulses from the body's extremities toward the central nervous system. Motor neurons are *efferent* neurons, which relay nerve impulses from the central nervous system toward the body's extremities.

Also keep in mind that the autonomic nervous system (ANS or visceral nervous system) is the part of the peripheral nervous system that acts as a control system functioning largely below the level of consciousness. It controls visceral functions, such as heart rate, digestion, respiration rate, salivation, perspiration, dilation of the pupils, urination, and sexual arousal. Whereas most of its actions are involuntary, some, such as breathing, work in tandem with the conscious mind.

The sympathetic nervous system serves an important function when we face danger, increasing one's heartbeat and blood pressure, along with other physiological changes. When we get stressed or face danger, the body releases cortisol. Cortisol makes you alert and attuned, ready to face the danger, but too much of it is not a good thing. With heightened cortisol levels, your muscles don't relax. Your insulin doesn't get released the way it should, so sugar turns to fat. You experience a craving for sweets. More sugar intake leads to more fat, which leads to ephaptic transmission or pain in your nerve endings. Your immunity is weakened.

When the stress is persistent or repetitive, the body keeps secreting cortisol, which puts an extra burden on the body. Signs and symptoms of long-term stress can include:

- Chronic headaches
- Mood swings
- Anxiety disorders
- Panic attacks
- Memory disturbance
- Weight loss
- Stomach ulcers
- Irritable bowel syndrome
- Exacerbation of allergies, including asthma
- Decreased sexual drive
- Sleeplessness
- Substance abuse
- Arrhythmias
- Heart attacks and strokes due increased blood pressure, sugar, cholesterol, and other factors.

Unlike short-term stress, the physical and physiological effects of long-term stress can continue to persist even after the stress triggers are no longer present (in the same way that chronic pain can persistently affect the body). In some cases, irreversible brain and organ damage can result.

Therefore, an increase in sympathetic activity, along with a decrease in parasympathetic activity, usually results in stress and, ultimately, tissue damage, due to decreases in circulation and hormonal imbalances (i.e., an increase or decrease in the level of various neurotransmitters and hormones, such as cortisol). Normal levels of neurotransmitters and hormones are essential for the normal functioning of the body, including the emotions and behaviors, but high levels have harmful effects on the body.

The Homeostatic Power of the Parasympathetic Nervous System

In contrast with the sympathetic nervous system, the parasympathetic nervous system relaxes the body by slowing the heart, dilating the blood vessels, and stimulating the digestive and genitourinary systems. The autonomic balancing power of the parasympathetic nervous system, with its ability to calm and heal the body, is the keystone of Ajrawat Air-Pulse Autonomic Therapy.

While the sympathetic nervous system is concerned with mobilizing the body to meet threats—it is the source of the well-known "fight or flight" syndrome—the parasympathetic nervous system (PNS) is concerned with relaxation and regeneration. When we're calm and at peace, the PNS is at work. One system stimulates us; the other sedates and calms us. While both are necessary to maintain normal human functioning (if the human race didn't respond to threats, it would be extinct today), the problem is that, in our modern world of stress and conflict, the SNS is overactive and over-stimulated, always on guard.

In a healthy organism, there is a state of balance. A threat appears. Our muscles become tense, our blood vessels constrict, our breathing becomes more rapid, our thoughts race. We need this heightened state of alert to pull a child away from traffic or to flee from a burning house.

But when the danger has passed, the parasympathetic nervous system should then take over. Our heartbeats and breathing should return to normal. Our blood vessels should relax and clear away metabolic waste products such as adrenaline and lactic acid. This is the normal balance of the human body: stress is followed by relaxation.

In the modern world, that balance has been upended. We worry constantly about money, our children, our relationships. It's a dog eat dog world, where only the strongest (or most ruthless) survive. Instead of compassion, beastly thoughts and the law of the jungle rule. We experience numerous conflicts and stresses in our life, almost on a constant basis, and the sympathetic nervous system constantly stays on guard, something it was never designed to do. We're in a constant state of alert, even though there may be no present or potential dangers facing us. Toxins and stress by-products build up in our bodies and are not released. Our muscles become ever more tense and contracted. We can never relax, never find inner peace, and we wonder why we have headaches, back pain, and heart conditions.

If the sympathetic nervous system has the perpetual upper hand, it will slowly become more and more difficult to relax. You get caught up in a vicious cycle of exhaustion, where you can't eat or sleep properly. Your thoughts race and tend to be negative. Add chronic pain to this equation, and you have a life of pure hell. It is little wonder that the body breaks down.

The power of Air-Pulse Autonomic Therapy is in its ability to calm the overactive sympathetic nervous system and to restore balance, harmony, and equilibrium between body and mind. It allows the body to regain homeostasis, so it can do its job properly. And, thanks to my invention, this can be achieved at any time, in any place, by any-one.

When we allow the PNS to have an equal prominence in our lives, life regains its expansive, open quality. Life will no longer feel tight and constricted, with few choices.

The PNS has the power to restore our peace of mind and well be-ing. We are able to enter another world we once experienced, but have long forgotten.

Air-Pulse Autonomic Therapy restores the prominence of the PNS, the home of all relaxing, warm, and contented feelings. It brings peace where there was conflict. It restores harmony and equilibrium. As Air-Pulse Autonomic Therapy relaxes muscles, blood vessels, and internal organs, the flow of all body fluids becomes easier, smoother, and full-er. The body begins to process the waste products that the sympathetic nervous system has created. The heartbeat slows and breathing deep-ens and softens. Autonomic Therapy changes the brain's waves and patterns, helping you achieve quieter, more expansive states of mind. Everything that has been strained becomes relaxed. Everything that has been contracted begins to expand. You regain the ability to get a good night's sleep and wake up refreshed. You have a new perspec-tive on life. You feel all your feelings, instead of denying them. You feel more creative, more giving, more in touch with yourself and oth-ers. The true potential of the brain is thus harnessed, and conscious-ness takes several leaps beyond our imagination.

And these benefits are not the result of religious belief or fan-tasy, but stem from basic scientific fact. By *lowering* sympathetic activity and *raising* the parasympathetic function, Ajrawat Air-Pulse Autonomic Therapy increases the production of neurotransmitters and hormones essential for normal emotional and behavioral responses. It initiates the process of reducing levels of cortisol, epinephrine, and nor-epinephrine in the blood, thus restoring autonomic balance to the body. It increases the levels of neurotransmitters like serotonin, acetylcholine, glutamate, dopamine, and others. As a result of the activation of the afferent mechanism, endorphins such as enkaphlin are produced, which in turn generate analgesia and a feeling of sedation.

In addition, Ajrawat Air-Pulse Autonomic Therapy not only restores lost homeostasis, but makes positive structural changes in neural tissue. This tissue, which has been damaged by physical or psychological trauma, such as PTSD, is healed. The limbic system, cingulate gyrus, pre-frontal cortex, basal ganglia, and left temporal lobe are just some of the structures in the brain that can be affected by physical trauma and stress, resulting in decreased circulation, neuronal atrophy, or damage resulting in hyper or hypoactivity, among other emotional and behavioral changes. Ajrawat Air-Pulse Autonomic Therapy heals this trauma, with startling and profound effects.

Hence, with discipline and regular utilization, Ajrawat Air-Pulse Autonomic Therapy can decondition and heal an unhealthy mind and body. As a bridge between conscious and unconscious processes in the body, it allows individuals to alter, in positive ways, basic bodily functions that have heretofore been considered beyond conscious control. We have the ability to lower our heart rates and blood pressure, balance neurotransmitters, release calming hormones, and repair damaged tissue. In a sequential, focused, and scientifically based manner, I realized I could help patients initiate a process that restored the body's homeostasis in a very short time. No recitation of mantras or playing of music was necessary in order to accomplish this desired relaxation and restoration of lost balance. Religious dogmas or beliefs did not get in the way. Patients could self-administer the therapy with ease.

This was a major breakthrough for me and a new invention was born, one that employed multiple components of the body—the nervous, cardiac, and respiratory systems—as well as one's sense of touch and ability to smile, all operating simultaneously. The ultimate goal is to focus on various organ and organ systems in combination, in order to generate and activate Dr. Ajrawat's Air-Pulse Homeostatic Reflex. This activates the mechanisms of the body's multiple reflex systems—central, somatic, and autonomic—to produce the desired central, somatic, and visceral effects, leading in turn to a balanced state of mind and body.

I believe that this self-administered cognitive medical therapy (also known as Khalistani Meditation Therapy) translates scientific facts about how the human mind and body function into a natural solution for various psychosomatic disorders, working from an entirely new frame of reference. It finally dispels as myth the long held scientific belief that the involuntary nervous system could not be altered at will. Hence, Ajrawat Air-Pulse Autonomic Therapy opens doors for new medical research in the fields of natural and integrative medicine.

In short, Ajrawat Air-Pulse Autonomic Therapy has the power to fundamentally transform the ways we understand and treat all forms of pain and stress

Meditation Therapy in Action

Perhaps you are still skeptical about the power of Ajrawat Air-Pulse Autonomic Therapy to help people deal with illness, stress, and pain. Can such a simple approach really help with those types of problems?

To answer this question, let's listen to a final case history in this chapter, the story of C.J.C., a type-1 diabetic who sought me out for treatment.

"Before implementing Dr. Ajrawat's meditation therapy into my daily routine, I was underweight and had no energy. I was smoking a pack of cigarettes a day and consuming about seven alcoholic drinks per week. I had lost my health almost completely. I felt beaten down and overwhelmed by the day-to-day pressures of life. My blood sugar levels were regularly in excess of 150 and controlling them seemed impossible. The only exercise I got was doing one pushup a day to get out of bed and bringing a cigarette to my lips. I was very pale and covered with patches of dry skin. I basically had given up on leading a healthy existence, barring a miracle.

"When Dr. Ajrawat introduced me to meditation therapy, I was very skeptical. How could something this simple help me with any of my issues? How could closing my eyes and feeling my pulse do anything to improve my life? I decided that I wasn't going to do anything different except add meditation to my day-to-day activities, to test how effective it would be. I had no confidence that it would be effective at all.

"Within two weeks of starting meditation therapy, my skepticism was gone. By meditating twice a day for 20 minutes, I began to notice big changes. I began to feel very balanced within myself, very controlled and calm. My energy increased to a level that I hadn't felt in years. My appetite came back, I regained a healthy looking color in my face, and waking up in the morning became easier day by day. To my extreme surprise, my blood sugar levels began to decrease without increasing either my insulin or exercise. I began to see that meditation was the miracle I was looking for.

"Over the next few months I was hospitalized with a lung infection brought on by my pack a day cigarette habit. I was faced with a very serious challenge—I had to stop smoking completely, immediately. I decided to try it cold turkey, because, thanks to meditation, I had a new feeling of empowerment and control. I also started a workout plan at this point that included running and lifting weights.

"The first week was pretty rough. I was craving a cigarette. But after that, the craving was completely gone and I haven't smoked a cigarette in the five months since. At the same time, I was also able to stop drinking alcohol with ease.

"At the present time, my weight is up to a healthy 153 pounds. I don't drink or smoke, and I feel mentally focused, physically energetic, positive, and stress free. My blood sugar levels average around 100 and I feel so much more alive than I have in the past 14 years. I never thought any of these changes would ever come to fruition. Now I carry a glow on my face, which was immediately noticed by my friends and family. My mother says that she has been amazed by my healthy appearance. Dr. Ajrawat's meditation therapy is the single most factor in my ability to regain a life that is balanced in every way."

Chapter 2

My Personal Journey as a Pain Management Specialist: Understanding Human Psychology, Conditioning, and Pain

My journey as a pain specialist has been a deeply personal one. I have dedicated my life to helping those who are suffering because of my own early experiences with emotional, physical, and cultural pain. By knowing a little about my background, you will understand how I have come to use my current treatment methods, and why I am so passionately committed to healing pain.

As a child growing up in the Punjab/Khalistan region of India, I was fascinated with the medical and academic professionals, which stimulated my desire to become a doctor.

My father, Dr. Pritam Singh, was a decorated World War Two veteran and a celebrated medical officer. He later became a pioneer anesthesiologist, having trained at the Yale University School of Medicine in the 1950s, and was subsequently dean of a medical school and vice president of the world federation of anesthesiologists. He often spoke about the wonders of the new field of anesthesia and how it would change the course of medical history, especially when it came to performing major surgical procedures like open heart surgery and organ transplants.

From an early age, I was exposed to medical practitioners and their ideas. I have a wonderful memory of Sir Dr. Robert Macintosh visiting our house for three days when I was eight years old. Dr. Macintosh was a world-renowned professor of anesthesia in Great Britain and Ireland. He had invented the famous technique of epidural anesthesia and analgesia, and was knighted for his achievements by the Queen of England. When I became a physician myself, I always was awed by this great technique, which helped millions, especially women in labor.

At age nine, I suffered an injury that had a profound affect on my life and later career as a pain management specialist. On a fall day we had taken a trip to the foothills of the Himalayas, to a place called Madhopur, for my father's medical school departmental picnic. At first the day went beautifully. Everyone was having fun, enjoying the great weather and beautiful view of the distant mountains. I decided to climb atop a nearby waterworks to take some snapshots of the jovial group. While climbing down, my foot slid and I landed face down on top of a large rock. I drifted in and out of consciousness during the two hours it took to reach the hospital. I suffered a concussion and fractured nose, and for many years thereafter experienced chronic neck pain.

Up to that time I had been a brilliant, outgoing, and perceptive child, but the head and neck trauma made it a little struggle, at times, to fully focus and concentrate in school. I have since done very well in my medical studies and career, but it wasn't easy to overcome the nasal bone damage and pain I suffered because of this blunt trauma.

I therefore developed an early understanding of and sympathy for the problem of long-term chronic pain. Those who suffer such pain are not an abstraction for me, but a visceral, living reality. That early injury also taught me a profound lesson about the fragility of the human body and brain—how a simple fall can affect one's emotional and physical health.

I was the youngest of four children growing up in a very disciplined and conservative household. My family loved me and cared for me, but at the same time I had to deal with verbal and emotional challenges in my environment. Silently and alone, I experienced some anxiety and pain. I tried various conservative treatments for my neck pain as a child and teenager, but nothing worked.

As I entered adulthood and studied hard for admission to medical school, I shifted my attention away from my pain. In simple terms, I gradually psyched myself into becoming stoical and indifferent towards my own suffering pain. I stayed away from all medication and kept myself engaged in sports and other activities. My mental and physical pain were somewhat alleviated over the years, but my struggle to become free from physical pain and associated stress, as well as to evolve into a fully realized individual, did not reach fruition until I invented and started practicing my own Air-Pulse Autonomic Therapy in the 1990s. Though I continue to suffer from low-level neck pain as a result of my childhood injuries, most of my mental, physical, and emotional pain is gone.

Though I was born free and determined as an individual, it was a tough struggle to fully realize my true self. With the help of my own meditation therapy and the famous and divine words of a Sikh Guru, Guru Gobind Singh ("Deh Siva Ber Mohe Eh Hai, Shubh Kerman Te Kabho Ho Na Taron…Nische Ker Apni Jeet Karon") or "Oh God grant me the boon that I am never deterred from doing good deeds… and with determination I achieve my victory"), I have succeeded in my quest to liberate myself from the burdens of emotional pain, and pain associated stress and anxiety. At the same time, I have helped patients from different background and faiths achieve the same mental freedom.

I can wholeheartedly echo the famous words of African-American civil rights leader Dr. Martin Luther King, Jr., who, while struggling for the freedom of a people enslaved for centuries, was able to say, "Free at last, free at last, thank God almighty, I am free at last."

I know in my heart that everyone has the ability to achieve that same freedom, and showing you the path to that goal is what this book is all about.

My Path to the Bio-Psychosocial Model

Dr. George Engel, a pioneer in his field, first introduced the bio-psychosocial model of illness in the 1970s. Engel's work was complemented by the multidisciplinary model of treating pain, invented by Dr. John J. Bonica, the father of modern pain management.

Both models recognize that biological, psychological, and sociological factors are interconnected in the cause and relief of pain. These models also recognize that psychosocial factors (such as beliefs, relationships, and stress) greatly impact the progression of and recuperation from illness and disease. In other words, these two models give us a much greater range of strategies and tools to diagnose and treat illness, and to help patients make full recoveries.

As Dr. Engel so eloquently stated:

> *To provide a basis for understanding the determinants of disease and arriving at rational treatments and patterns of health care, a medical model must also take into account the patient, the social context in which he lives, and the complementary system devised by society to deal with the disruptive effects of illness—that is, the physician's role and the health care system.*

In 1983 I had the opportunity to meet Dr. John Bonica at an international pain conference in Italy. He became an instant friend. Dr. Bonica had wrestled professionally in his youth, suffered from chronic pain as a result, and had undergone multiple hip surgeries. To hear about his personal experience with pain, as well as his pioneer methods for treating it, was a revelation and turning point in my personal and professional life. Dr. Bonica, who introduced pain management some years ago, was now striving to make it into a full-fledged discipline. He founded the International Association for the Study of Pain (IASP), which, in 1979, presented the first official definition of pain, to be discussed in the next chapter.

I was trained in the bio-psychosocial model of illness and the multidisciplinary model of treating pain during my fellowship in pain management at the University of Texas Health Sciences Center in San Antonio, Texas, where I studied with pioneer pain specialist Dr. S. Ramamurthy. I was trained in a multidisciplinary pain management center, where under one roof various disciplines were used in tandem to evaluate and manage pain. I not only learned various physical skills and techniques to treat it, but also gained the necessary theoretical knowledge to develop new approaches and techniques.

After finishing my fellowship training I moved to the Washington, D.C. area, where I opened the region's first model pain management center in July 1985. I was both determined and excited to bring about fundamental changes that could benefit many thousands of pain and stress sufferers.

Two years earlier, I had attended a lecture on pain at a meeting of the American Society of Anesthesiologists in Atlanta, Georgia. Dr. Stephen Abrams, a pioneer pain specialist, made a presentation in which he tried to distinguish between cancerous and non-cancerous pain, calling the latter "benign pain." Dr. Bonica, who had suffered severe hip pain and undergone multiple surgeries himself, said in response that no pain could be called benign, as he personally knew what pain could do to the individual. He added that pain would one day be treated through meditation therapy. I was intrigued by that comment and, as a resident in anesthesia, became convinced that what he said could have profound ramifications for healing the many facets of pain. Today, 27 years later, I believe that moment has arrived with my invention of Ajrawat Air-Pulse Autonomic Therapy.

From the start, my Washington Pain Management Center operated from a specialized, interdisciplinary, conservative, and patient-centered approach that addresses all components of chronic pain simultaneously, including pain-associated stress. In the forefront of my practice are new diagnostic techniques, which I use to address problems that, under traditional models of treatment, have been commonly misdiagnosed, such as herniated disc syndrome, myofascial pain disorder (often misdiagnosed as arthritis of the spine and knees), myofascial entrapment neuropathies, myofascial headaches (which are often misdiagnosed as migraines), and myofascial pain, which is often overlooked and very seldom treated appropriately.

Through a close study of a patient's medical history and an exhaustive physical examination, supplemented by lab tests, scans, and other non-invasive tests, I am able to provide an accurate diagnosis of a person's condition, often for the first time in the patient's history. My diagnosis includes complementary and perpetuating factors that the majority of doctors ignore, such as variations in limb length, rounded shoulders, heavy breasts in females, poor head and neck posture during sleep, faulty posture, and faulty gait. The pioneering work of Dr. Janet Travell in understanding and treating myofascial pain was a great help in providing effective care to my patients. Improperly designed bifocal lenses can cause headaches, while a tight belt around the waist and thick wallets can cause back and leg pain, and carrying a purse or bag over the shoulder can cause neck or shoulder pain. These conditions are often exacerbated by poorly designed furniture at work and home, such as an inadequate office chair, or a mattress that is soft and of poor quality.

When it comes to complementary factors, skeletal disproportion is a serious but often overlooked cause of chronic pain. When Waleed, age 12, came to see me, he had been suffering chronic pain throughout his body for almost five years. Waleed couldn't run, jump, do any type of exercises, or even walk without feeling pain. He became depressed and worried. His parents took him to a number of doctors, who prescribed various medicines, but without relief. Finally Waleed's father brought him to see me.

I examined him thoroughly, observed how he walked, and ordered some x-rays. I determined that one of Waleed's legs was shorter than the other. At first he was heartbroken, but then I explained to him that this was a very common problem. It didn't mean that he was incapable of doing normal activities. After going through my treatment plan, Waleed's pain was alleviated, and he can now run, jump, and do just about anything without discomfort. And he is not depressed anymore.

In addition, my patients are motivated to use correct nutrition, maintain an ideal weight, engage in strengthening and stretching exercises, and to alternate walking and jogging on a daily basis to restore lost stamina and strength.

Human Psychology, Conditioning, and Pain

In the following chapters I will describe in detail how each aspect of my treatment program works, including a close look at Ajrawat Air-Pulse Autonomic Therapy, but first I would like to say more about how our fears, emotions, and behaviors figure in pain management and relief. This is a basic tenet of the bio-psychosocial model and the foundation of my approach, which is based on the understanding that it is impossible to treat the body in isolation from the mind, and that the nexus between the two can never be underestimated.

Physical and emotional pain are deeply, intrinsically connected. Thanks to new technology and research, we know that the same part of the brain that processes physical pain—the anterior cingulate cortex— also processes emotional pain. When the body experiences stress, the anterior cingulate cortex increases the activity of the vagus nerve, which connects your brain stem to your neck, chest, and abdomen. That is why we often feel butterflies or nausea when we experience stress.

And just as physical pain can be chronic and long lasting, so, too, can emotional pain. Anyone who has suffered through the loss of a loved one, a divorce, or the failure of one's physical health knows that fact all too well.

Though human beings are considered the most advanced and sophisticated of all creatures on planet earth, we are also the most vulnerable. And that is because, unlike other creatures on this planet, we are not only physically vulnerable, but emotionally and psychologically vulnerable as well. This is especially true at the extremes of experience, when we are confronted by harsh environments and difficult circumstances. In short, human consciousness is capable of being injured in multiple ways. We can suffer long lasting emotional and physical damage after a loved one dies; we can also experience the same kind of damage after a friend speaks to us harshly or someone gives us a nasty look. Human emotions (and brain chemistry, as you will soon see) can be very fragile, which complicates the correct diagnosis and treatment of pain.

In addition to our innate fragility, our conditioning (religious, family, and cultural) has a profound impact on how we experience pain and how we recover from it (or whether we recover at all). I believe a major cause of stress or psychological problems is conditioning that distorts one's free will and true identity. It is well known that human beings are vulnerable to covert manipulation. For example, people's minds can be controlled by spells, trances, mesmerism, and hypnosis without their consent or conscious awareness. We know this often happens in a religious or cult setting—there are countless examples of such mass conditioning throughout history. Hitler and Nazi Germany are the modern day examples, besides more subtle ones.

Most religions consider love, equality, the practice of correct principles, and the empowerment of others to be great qualities. Yet we often witness millions of human beings following religious belief systems blindly, never questioning their true validity. We learn from history that religious people who are self-righteous and overzealous cause great pain and suffering, for the victim as well the innocent bystander. The vast majority of these doctrines or philosophies only lead to more confusion and stress, which can further limit the realization of one's own abilities and potential.

Until now, the term "meditation therapy" has been synonymous with religious philosophy and personal "salvation." That has unfortunately led to a flourishing of holy men and gurus from both east and west, who have exploited the public's trust to advance their own agenda, whether it be mind control of their followers or financial gain. One example is Ridhi and Sidhis, the old Indian practice of occult power and mind control. In the west, the control of people's minds through religious illusions and imaginary visions has had disastrous consequences. The end result has been the loss of one's identity, lack of homeostasis in mind and body, and more stress and disease. This has not only led to a submissive, subdued, and negatively conditioned state of mind amongst major groups of people, but has also turned people against one another. Religious philosophy has warped people's perceptions of their fellow human beings, leading to condemnation of them as unworthy sinners without any basis in fact.

Whole groups of people have been labeled "heathens" or "infidels" out of sheer self-righteousness and so-called religious or racial superiority. Such attitudes lead to the death and destruction of millions in the world. In India, religious-based conditioning and the manipulation of human beings in a degrading caste system have led to unbelievable suffering and pain. The low caste or black untouchables (Dalits) have been treated worse than animals by the so-called "high caste" Brahmins. The pain and suffering caused by this mental tyranny and terrorism have destroyed the psyches and self esteem of generations of innocent, poor, yet perfectly normal human beings. A subtler yet still enslaving tyranny lures the poor and helpless into certain religious belief systems. All tyrannies, whether mental or physical, lead to pain, suffering, and loss of homeostatic balance.

The tyrant Hitler could not have risen to power without mass conditioning based on hate, bigotry, and racial superiority. What is less appreciated is that such manipulation can also occur in any group setting, including the family. A dysfunctional family can have a profound impact on its members. People who are very trusting, highly suggestible, or who have low self-esteem are particularly vulnerable. Devastating psychological and psychiatric effects can result from being in the company of an abusive or manipulative parent or person, a narcissistic sibling, or an alcoholic parent. Prolonged contact with such people can lead to a faulty frame of reference and ultimately result in devastating behaviors or outcomes in one's life. Certain psychologically devised and deliberated gestures or manners have been very effective in controlling, manipulating or enslaving the human mind, especially in the western world. Bending the wrist gently and extending the hand flaccidly while shaking hands with someone; or smiling while rolling the eyes downwards have been very sophisticated and effective ways of harming people's self esteem. Such psychophysical maneuvers have been instrumental in creating hierarchies, projecting a false sense of superiority, and mentally enslaving people for generations. Thank God these tactics are gradually fading, as the world is becoming more educated and aware.

And while damage can be caused by alcoholism or sexual abuse or neglect, lesser evils can also cause profound problems. Something as simple as a nasty facial expression can affect one's self-image and self-esteem. Negative conditioning in the family can become a huge impediment to a person reaching his or her fullest potential. Depression and anxiety can become conditioned realities that exist throughout one's lifetime and get passed down from one generation to the next.

In addition to family conditioning, there is also cultural conditioning. I have an intimate understanding of how an entire cultural group can experience and pass down pain over many generations. I grew up as a religious Sikh in India. As the member of a persecuted and disenfranchised ethnic minority, I have witnessed firsthand the suffering that can be inflicted on a minority by a majority. Sikhs have never forced their will on others, but neither have they allowed others to inflict their wills upon them. As a result, they have endured much suffering throughout history.

Sikhs underwent three major holocausts, two at the hands of invading Islamic Mughals in 1730 and 1760, and another at the hands of Hindu and Gujjar mobs in 1984. In 1730, more than 10,000 Sikhs were massacred in a day, and 30 years later the tyrant Ahmed Shah Abdali massacred 30,000 more. This was a devastating setback for the Sikh religion, as we were only few in numbers at that time.

In 1849, the Sikhs lost their geopolitical sovereignty and empire to the British. Their property, including the diamond Kohinoor, was confiscated. Their minor prince, Maharaja Duleep Singh, was brought to England at age 13 by Lord Dalhousie on the orders of Queen Victoria. Victoria, a German by descent, belonging to House of Hanover, forcefully converted him to Christianity. The loss of the homeland was, and continues to be, a trauma suffered by each individual Sikh and by the Sikh culture as a whole. The conversion of their sovereign to another religion against his free will is the worst type of religious oppression and persecution that can be committed by the sovereign of one nation against the sovereign of another. This was all done to gain more power and control. The end result has been pain and suffering for millions of people who belong to an ecumenical religion and egalitarian society, and who saved the Hindu religion from extinction by turning back the onslaught of invading Mughals.

It was subsequently very ironic that the Sikhs, at great personal sacrifice, helped save the sovereignty of the British and French, when they fought on their sides as allies against the Germans in the First World War and against the Nazis in the Second World War. When India sought freedom from the British, 86% of the freedom fighters who went to the gallows were Sikhs, although they made up only 2% of the population. It was the Sikhs who brought an end to African slave trading in Malawi in 1893. It was the Sikh leadership that righteously recognized Israel's right to exist in 1948, when so many other nations did not, including India, which did not recognize the Jewish state until 1992 and only under pressure from rest of the world. I often wonder why human beings treat each other with such indifference and disgrace. The only way the Sikh nation's pain, suffering, and lost homeostatic and geopolitical balance can be restored is through reclamation of its lost sovereignty. While Sikhs continue to struggle to achieve that goal, the English, French, and Indians owe it to the Sikh nation to restore that balance, based on the personal sacrifices Sikhs made for their countries. To know more about the Sikh struggle for the reclamation of lost geopolitical sovereignty, please visit Khalistan.net.

In 1984, more than 4,000 Sikhs were burnt alive in Delhi alone by Hindu and Gujjar mobs after Indira Gandhi's assassination. Indian police and para-military forces, between 1984 and 1999, have massacred more than 350,000 Sikhs. To this day, the guilty have gone unpunished. The only way to bring relief and closure of this type of pain is by bringing the guilty to justice. And yet that closure has not been achieved.

More than 65 years ago, the world witnessed the Jewish Holocaust. More than six million were sent to the gas chambers by the greatest tyrant of modern times. All of us have seen documentaries of that genocide. Those who survived that ordeal truly know the definition of pain and suffering. The genocide victim and his progeny know the existential fear of being extinct one day. During my work at Montefiore Hospital of the Albert Einstein College of Medicine in New York City, I acquired an intimate knowledge of that suffering through my contact with descendants of victims of the Holocaust.

My wife had a friend named Ms. Stein, whose grandmother had survived the Holocaust. Once, as a child, Ms. Stein asked her grandmother why she overfed her and the other grandchildren. Her grandmother didn't answer and Ms. Stein persisted in her questioning.

Finally, the grandmother broke her silence:

"Honey, I overfeed you because one day you might have to fall back on that extra weight in order to survive."

When my wife told me this story, I was outraged. Because of my familiarity with numerous persecutions in Sikh history, I felt as if someone had put a noose around my neck. At the same time, I felt I had to undo that noose and take on the tyrants with all the force at my disposal. I affirmed that day that there would never be another Holocaust during my lifetime. I aspire to help make this world a better place, where we must live by the principles of love and pleasure and not pain. We must live and let others live, and never submit to tyranny.

Having personally witnessed the Sikh Holocaust of 1984, I have lived for many years with deeply felt pain, stress, and anger. Therefore, as a pain specialist, I empathize with all who want their sovereignty restored, be they Palestinians, Tibetans, or Kurds, so long they affirm the correct principles of live and let live. It is only through mutual consideration and righteousness that we can restore homeostatic balance between whole peoples and nations.

The point to remember is that it is difficult if not impossible for the average individual to understand the threat a minority people faces—the threat of being wiped from the face of this planet. As a pain specialist, I fully understand how such fears can condition the minds and bodies of an entire people through succeeding generations. Such traumas not only evoke the "fight or flight" response, but also throw the body's entire system into a reactive and defensive mode. The body wants to live in harmony with itself and nature. Our human instinct struggles to maintain homeostatic balance within and without. Yet, when a person experiences pain on either an individual or cultural basis, that balance becomes very difficult to restore.

From childhood I was groomed to do good deeds as best as I could and help the needy. Yet I was also raised according to Sikh tenets to be a soldier as well as a saint—to never yield to the tyrant or those who inflict pain on others. I believe everyone should embody the dual qualities of saint and soldier. You must be a saint when your environment is peaceful, and a soldier when your environment becomes harsh and dangerous and warrants action.

Because of their painful sagas of persecution, Sikhs learned this dual approach. Its Gurus (divine teachers), as well as millions of regular Sikhs, were persecuted not because they attempted to impose their faith on others, but simply because they refused to submit to self-righteous tyranny.

After the second holocaust of 1760 we reunited, and two months later we attacked and kicked the Mughals out of our homeland forever. The Sikhs made a statement for all mankind, showing that it was possible to endure pain and suffering for a righteous cause, to attain a balance between mind and body, and to maintain one's self respect and dignity. We showed the world that it was righteous and principled to be both a saint and a soldier.

The tyrant will continue to force his will on innocent mankind until the sword of righteous force challenges him. The imbalance in homeostasis has to be restored on a worldwide basis in order for all the earth's inhabitants to function in a healthy and harmonious manner.

Human Freedom Demands a New Paradigm

The important point is to recognize the all-pervasive nature of pain, which affects our thoughts, attitudes, emotions, and behavior. In turn, our thoughts, attitudes, emotions, and behavior affect how we react to and recover from pain.

That is because there is not only a biological basis for physical pain, but also a biological basis for emotional pain and depression. That suffering leads to an imbalance in neurotransmitters and hormones, as well as damage to certain important parts of the brain, such as the hypothalamus, the pre-frontal cortex, and left temporal lobe, among others. In other words, there is a biological basis for the madness we see in the world. Faulty conditioning, impaired brain circuitry, and the loss of homeostasis can lead to psychopathic behaviors, culminating in wars, great disasters, and other assorted curses upon humanity. The history of mankind is full of such imbalances, on both an individual and cultural basis.

I've described how scientists believe that emotional pain and emotional disorders result from an excess of neurotransmitters and other neurochemicals in the brain. When this happens, the neurons cannot release enough neurotransmitter molecules to excite the rest of the nervous system, and symptoms of depression occur. At the same time, neurons can become toxic. When they release toxins, these substances can over-excite the nervous system, creating symptoms ranging from mild anxiety, to mania and extreme acts of violence.

In other words, depression is a toxic situation built up over time in the brain's neurons, sometimes beginning as early as childhood. The chemicals and neurotransmitters affected cannot perform their functions well enough to bring the person out of depression. Eventually, the neurons become too toxic and need to detoxify. As they do so, they flood the nervous system with neurotransmitters, overexciting what was once under-excited.

This creates a dilemma for the human mind to be truly free and self-empowered. If our emotional conditioning has physical, brain-based roots, it cannot be healed by the same systems that caused that conditioning—religion, culture, family, or traditional therapy. Those institutions and approaches have value, but not in addressing the problems they have created. For, as in the words of Albert Einstein, "A significant problem created at one level of thinking cannot be solved at the same level of thinking."

Therefore, better approaches are needed to understand the functioning of mind and body, their detours from normalcy, the increasing incidence of mental and physical diseases in modern times, and the ever-growing challenges posed by the speed and pressures of modern life. Our social systems are going through incredible changes and, in the famous words of Dr. Jonas Salk, "It is the survival of the wisest."

We must meet this challenge head on, through new approaches that combine the best of ancient practices with solid reasoning and modern scientific logic. Such approaches can pave the way for greater understanding of new realities and for forging a better human existence. I believe that Ajrawat Air-Pulse Autonomic Therapy is one such approach. My invention holds great promise for individuals who suffer from all kinds of medical, psychiatric, and pain disorders. Yet healthy individuals can greatly benefit from my medical therapy as well.

Because it is scientifically-based and non-denominational, it frees people from the burdens of environment, family, and religious dogma, while creating psychological and emotional health through the natural healing process of the body, which every one of us has access to. Ajrawat Air-Pulse Autonomic Therapy offers an entirely new paradigm for addressing ancient human problems in natural, non-intrusive ways, by going to the heart of the problem—restoring the body's and brain's lost homeostasis.

How Ajrawat Air-Pulse Autonomic
Meditation Therapy Affects Brain Chemistry

What does that quote of Einstein's mean, and how is it related to Ajrawat Meditation Therapy?

My answer: "If old ways of thinking have gotten us into the problem, more old thinking will not get us out." In other words, if psychological and emotional pain have physical origins, if, in short, they are linked to changes in brain chemistry and the connection between mind and body, then traditional approaches, whether medical or meditative, that ignore these connections and relations will not work.

Until now, it has been believed that psychological or psychiatric illnesses were primarily the result of one's environment, psychological makeup, and genetic disposition. Hence psychoanalysis, psychotherapy, and medication were considered the major ways of treating these disorders.

But now, with better research and technology, a fundamental shift is taking place. It was not until the early 1980s that research in Europe and the U.S. started pointing in the direction of structural changes in the brain and body, especially in the imbalance of neurotransmitters and hormones. As a result of thorough clinical evaluation and newer diagnostic techniques, such as MRI scans, functional MRI scans, SPECT scans, and PET scans, we have learned that brain chemistry has a profound impact on our thoughts, emotions, and behavior.

It has become accepted scientific fact that changes in neurobiology in important structures of the brain (such as the limbic system, basal ganglia, cingulate gyrus, hypothalamus, amygdala, left temporal cortex, pre frontal cortex, and others) can lead to cognitive, emotional, behavioral, and mood changes, and eventually to the development of specific psychological disorders. Changes in the anatomy and physiology of particular brain structures can produce specific symptoms and signs of emotional problems.

As a pain specialist by training, I have long understood how various parts of the brain play important roles in the perception, interpretaion, and encephalization of pain and stress. Seeing patients in my practice with many different physical, psychological, and psychiatric manifestations has helped me relate to various symptoms and signs in a more empathic manner. What I knew earlier in my career and learned later based on ongoing research helped me formulate a better treatment plan and led to the subsequent development of my meditation therapy.

It is important to know the physiological functioning of the various parts of the brain, though I must point out that science continues to change and new research brings new findings. But we must be willing to change our knowledge and make our goals more refined without becoming dogmatic. Based on the most recent research, here are examples of how changes in particular parts of the brain affect emotions and behavior.

Deep Limbic System: moodiness, irritability, depression.

Basal Ganglia: primarily involved in anxiety, panic attacks, worrying, myofascial pain.

Cingulate Gyrus: obsessive and compulsive behavior, eating disorders, compulsive addictive behavior, and oppositional behavior.

Temporal Lobe: left temporal lobe involvement can lead to aggression, violent thoughts, emotional instability, memory problems, and amnesia.

Amugdala: fear and panic attacks.

Pre-Frontal Cortex: hyperactivity, distractability, short attention span, poor judgment, impulse control problems, and other problems.

Head trauma can also alter one's emotions and behaviors. Having been trained in surgery and as an anesthesiologist and pain specialist, I have treated a number of patients whose affect and behavior changed because of such trauma.

Head trauma is commonly caused by motor vehicle accidents, falls, playing sports like boxing and football, and assaults. You're at greater risk if you're female, have a poor social support network, or suffer from depression. Depression and PTSD often are co-symptoms of head trauma. Repeated mild brain injuries can result in cumulative neurologic and cognitive deficits. After suffering a concussion, a variety of symptoms can appear, ranging from mild and transient, to severe, ongoing, and disabling.

Head trauma symptoms include: headaches, neck pain, dizziness/light headedness, sensitivity to noise and light, anxiety/irritability, depression, fatigue, insomnia, drowsiness, nausea/vomiting, confusion, memory problems, slurred speech, blurred vision, and physical imbalance.

Symptoms of injuries to the frontal lobe include impulsivity and disinhibition, blunted affect, emotional and/or social withdrawal, passivity, lack of spontaneity, aggression, outbursts of rage and violent behavior, apathy and disorganization, attention and memory deficits, mood disregulation, impaired social judgment, uncharacteristic lewdness, inability to appreciate the effects of one's own behavior or remarks on others, impaired communication skills, loss of social graces, diminution of attention to personal appearance and hygiene, and boisterousness.

The good news is that brain chemistry can be also altered for the greater good.

Ajrawat Air-Pulse Autonomic Therapy is an effective treatment for all disorders resulting from the hyper or hypo activity of these various regions. It helps restore the normalcy of brain functioning by:

- Restoring the homeostatic balance between the sympathetic and parasympathetic nervous systems.
- Activating the afferent input that helps improve circulation to these areas through vasodilatation.
- Initiating the Air-Pulse Homeostatic Reflex, which improves circulation in the entire body, including the brain, intestines, heart, and other parts of the body.
- Restoring various neurotransmitters to normal levels, including Serotonin, Acetylcholine, Glutamate, Dopamine, and others.
- Breaking the negative circuitry in the brain, resulting from previous noxious and non-noxious sensory inputs.

Just calming the mind, as in traditional therapy, is not enough. By activating the body's natural healing systems and restoring balance in brain chemistry, Ajrawat Air-Pulse Autonomic Therapy offers us a chance to overcome negative conditioning on an individual, family, and cultural level.

Chapter 3

Ajrawat Air-Pulse Autonomic Therapy and Brain Chemistry: The Foundations of a New Paradigm

In order to understand how I treat pain, whether it's the emotional pain of stress and anxiety, or chronic physical pain in the back, neck, or shoulder, let's spend a little time understanding exactly what pain is. The International Association for the Study of Pain (IASP) defines pain as follows:

Pain is an unpleasant emotional and sensory experience associated with actual or potential tissue damage. (IASP 1979)

That means that pain, especially chronic pain, is not a uni-dimensional problem, but rather a complex multidimensional problem that has many components or attributes. Note that, according to this definition, pain is not merely experienced physically (or somatically) in the body, but also emotionally. Also note that pain is associated with either *actual or potential* tissue damage. That means the perception of pain is real, whether or not actual damage is occurring. For example, there is the phenomenon of phantom limb pain, where a person can experience pain in a missing limb. The fact that pain is multidimensional has profound emotional and behavioral consequences, as well as physical consequences, for human beings.

To fully understand the multidimensional aspects of pain, we need to understand how the body functions.

The term integration refers to how the systems of the human body function and overlap. Like any system, the human body functions through communication, which occurs in both electrical and chemical ways. Without communication, there is no integration and therefore no proper functioning of the body.

For example, the endocrine and nervous systems play major roles in the reception and transmission of signals, which integrate the functioning of the body. When systems in the body are communicating and functioning properly, homeostasis occurs. Homeostasis is the proper regulation of an internal environment, which in the case of humans means the maintenance of stable and constant conditions in the body.

Homeostatic regulation maintains normal body temperature and regulates blood glucose levels, which helps prevent hyperglycemia. When insulin is deficient or cells become resistant to it, diabetes occurs. The kidneys also perform a vital role in homeostatic regulation, removing excess water, salt, and urea from the blood. These waste projects are then expelled as urine.

When homeostasis is disturbed (a condition known as "homeostatic imbalance"), disease can result. When the body temperature rises or the kidneys don't function, damage to the body can result. Aging can also upset homeostatic balance. Every organism, when it ages, loses efficiency in its control systems, and the human body is no exception. These inefficiencies lead to an unstable internal environment that increases the risk for illness. The physical changes associated with aging are also the result of homeostatic imbalance.

All systems of the body are involved in maintaining homeostasis, such as the nervous system, the circulatory system, the respiratory system, and the endocrine system, among others. Let's take a closer look at two of these systems: the nervous system and the endocrine system.

Understanding the Human Nervous System

The nervous system is composed of two main parts, the central nervous system, which is made up of the brain and the spinal cord, and the peripheral nervous system, which is made up of the sensory and motor nerves. Picture it this way: the brain and spinal cord occupy central positions in the body, while the sensory and motor nerves extend throughout the body.

The central nervous system (CNS) consists of the brain and the spinal cord, and is the part of the nervous system that coordinates the activity of all parts of the body. Together with the peripheral nervous system, it has a fundamental role in the control of behavior.

The peripheral nervous system (PNS) consists of the nerves and ganglia outside of the brain and the spinal cord. The main function of the PNS is to connect the CNS to the limbs and organs of the body. Unlike the central nervous system, the PNS is not protected by the cranium or the vertebral canal, leaving it relatively exposed to toxins and mechanical injuries. The peripheral nervous system is further divided, functionally as well as structurally, into the somatic nervous system and the autonomic nervous system.

The somatic nervous system (SNS) is the part of the peripheral nervous system associated with the voluntary control of body movements through the action of skeletal muscles and with reception of external stimuli, which help keep the body in touch with its surroundings (e.g., touch, hearing, and sight). It is the system that regulates activities that are under conscious control. The SNS includes all neurons connected with skeletal muscles, skin, and sense organs. The somatic nervous system consists of efferent nerves responsible for sending brain signals for muscle contraction.

Note, as stated before, that there are two types of neurons, carrying nerve impulses in different directions:

- The sensory neurons are *afferent* neurons, which relay nerve impulses *toward* the brain from the outer reaches of the body.
- The motor neurons are *efferent* neurons, which relay nerve impulses *from* brain toward the outer reaches of the body.

In contrast to the somatic nervous system, the autonomic nervous system (ANS or visceral nervous system) is the part of the peripheral nervous system that acts as a control system functioning largely *below* the level of consciousness. It controls visceral functions, such as heart rate, digestion, respiration rate, salivation, perspiration, dilation of the pupils, urination, and sexual arousal. Whereas most of its actions are involuntary, some, such as breathing, work in tandem with the conscious mind.

The autonomic nervous system is then further divided into the sympathetic division, parasympathetic division, and enteric division.

The sympathetic nervous system responds to impending danger, and is responsible for the corresponding increase in one's heartbeat and blood pressure, among other physiological changes, along with the sense of excitement one feels due to the increase of adrenaline in the system. The parasympathetic nervous system, on the other hand, is evident when a person is resting and feels relaxed, and is responsible for such things as the constriction of the pupils, the slowing of the heart, the dilation of the blood vessels, and the stimulation of the digestive and genitourinary systems. The role of the enteric nervous system is to manage every aspect of digestion, from the esophagus to the stomach, small intestine, and colon.

The nervous system is composed of a network of neurons and other supportive cells (such as glial cells). A neuron (also known as a nerve cell) is an electrically excitable cell that processes and transmits information by electrical and chemical signaling. Chemical signaling occurs via synapses or specialized connections with other cells. Neurons connect to each other to form networks or functional circuits, each responsible for specific tasks. Neurons are the core components of the nervous system. A number of specialized types of neurons exist. As described before, sensory neurons respond to touch, sound, light, and numerous other stimuli, affecting cells of the sensory organs, which then send signals to the spinal cord and brain. Motor neurons receive signals from the brain and spinal cord, and cause muscle contractions and affect glands. Interneurons connect neurons to other neurons within the same region of the brain or spinal cord.

Keep in mind that neurons carry nerve impulses in different directions in the body, a biological fact that plays a key role in how I treat pain. Again, sensory neurons are *afferent* neurons, which relay nerve impulses from the body's extremities toward the central nervous system. Motor neurons are *efferent* neurons, which relay nerve impulses from the central nervous system toward the body's extremities.

Thus, neuroscience can be studied at many different levels, ranging from the molecular level to the cellular level, the systems level, and cognitive level. All levels play a vital role in how the body experiences pain, and to what degree it can recover from its affects.

Understanding the Human Endocrine System

The endocrine system, like the nervous system, plays a large role in maintaining homeostasis in the body. Like the nervous system, the endocrine system is an information signal system. Through a system of glands, each of which secretes a type of hormone into the bloodstream, it regulates many functions, including mood, growth and development, tissue function, and metabolism.

The endocrine system is made up of a series of ductless glands that produce chemicals called hormones. Typical endocrine glands are the pituitary, thyroid, and adrenal glands. Glands that signal each other in sequence are usually referred to as an axis, as, for example, the hypothalamic-pituitary-adrenal axis.

The thyroid gland plays an extremely important role in the regulation of the body's metabolism and other functions. Low levels of thyroid hormones often lead to a decrease in one's pain threshold and the production of myofascial pain. In addition, such an imbalance can lead to depression, fatigue, weakness, hair loss, cold intolerance, irritability, memory loss, dry skin, weight gain, and an abnormal menstrual cycle.

In addition to the specialized endocrine organs mentioned above, many other organs that are part of other body systems, such as the kidneys, liver, heart, and gonads, have secondary endocrine functions. For example, the kidneys secrete endocrine hormones such as erythropoietin and renin.

The secretion of various hormones from the endocrine system initiates the process of reducing levels of other hormones in the body, such as cortisol, epinephrine, and nor-epinephrine in the blood, thus restoring autonomic balance to the body. As a result of the afferent mechanism, endorphins such as enkaphlins are produced, which in turn generate analgesia and a feeling of sedation.

Thus, like the nervous system, the endocrine system plays a key role in regulating homeostasis in the body.

Understanding Brain Chemistry

Now that we understand how the nervous and endocrine systems work, let's take a look at brain chemistry, which is fundamental to how the body experiences and processes pain.

More than one hundred chemicals circulate in the brain and are known as neurochemicals or neurotransmitters. Four of these neurochemical systems are considered especially crucial in how our brains and bodies function: norepinephrine, serotonin, dopamine, and acetylcholine. A lack or overabundance of these neurochemicals is associated with various neuropsychiatric illnesses. For example, Parkinson's disease seems to be related to a lack of dopamine at the base of the brain, while lower acetylcholine levels are associated with Alzheimer's dementia. Dopamine affects addictive disorders. Consumption of drugs and alcohol releases dopamine in the brain, which leads to feelings of euphoria. The dopamine system becomes desensitized through habitual drug or alcohol abuse, which means that the substance abuser has to use more drugs or alcohol to achieve a high. This creates the cycle of addiction: the addict has to take more drugs to achieve the same desired high, and becomes increasingly debilitated and depressed.

Imbalances of dopamine and serotonin in certain areas of the brain are associated with schizophrenia. Finally, the depressive disorders appear to be associated with lowered levels of serotonin and norepinephrine. It's important to understand that scientists and researchers don't really know whether low levels of neurochemicals in the brain cause depression or whether depression causes low levels of neurochemicals in the brain. At any rate, there is an association between the two.

To sum up, serotonin modulates mood, satiety (satisfaction in appetite), and sleeping patterns; dopamine modulates reward-seeking behavior, pleasure, and maternal/paternal and altruistic feelings; norepinephrine determines levels of alertness, danger perception, and fight-or-flight responses; and acetylcholine controls memory and cognition processes.

In addition, gamma amino butyric acid (GABA) is an important mood regulator because it controls and inhibits chemical changes in the brain during stress.

Nerve cells pass signals to each other by means of neurotransmitters. Neurotransmitters are composed of simple amino acids, such as glutamate. After the signal is passed to the next neuron, glutamate is then swiftly cleared from the nerve cell junctions to keep the message brief. However, when the messages are overwhelming, as in a stroke or epilepsy, glutamate is not cleared from the nerve cells, and this prolonged excitation is toxic to nerve cells, apparently due to calcium flooding the cell. Nerve cells can be damaged or even destroyed. For example, abundant evidence points to glutamate as a destructive factor in ALS (Amyotrophic lateral sclerosis, a disease of the nerve cells in the brain and spinal cord).

Chronic stress or highly traumatic experiences cause adaptive or compensatory changes in brain neurochemistry and physiology, in order to provide the individual with defense and survival mechanisms. However, such adaptive changes come with a high cost, in particular when they are required for an extended period, such as in war zones or other prolonged stressful situations. The adaptive chemicals tend to outlast the situation for which they were required, leading to some form of affective and behavioral disorder.

These adaptive neurochemical changes are especially harmful during early childhood. For instance, children who have been neglected or abused physically, sexually, or emotionally are exposed to harmful levels of glucocorticoids (comparable to those found in war veterans) that lead to neuron atrophy (wasting) and cropping (reduced numbers) in the hippocampus region of the brain. This can result in cognitive and memory disorders, anxiety, and poor emotional control. Neuronal cropping also occurs in the frontal cortex of the brain's left hemisphere, leading to fewer nerve-cell connections with several other brain areas. These decreased nerve-cell connections favor epilepsy-like short circuits or microseizures in the brain that occur in association with bursts of aggressiveness, self-destructive behavior, and cognitive or attention disorders. These alterations are also seen in the brains of adults who were abused or neglected during childhood. Length of exposure and severity of suffered abuse help determine the extent of brain damage and the severity of psychiatric-related disorders in later stages of life. Mechanical stressors, such as head trauma from playing sports or hitting a hard surface, like a floor or a wall, can lead to behavioral and emotional problems later in life. Head trauma can lead to structural damage in certain parts of the brain, such as the prefrontal cortex and temporal lobe, which in turn commonly cause attention deficit disorder and other emotional and behavioral changes.

Therefore, there is a profound relationship between brain chemistry and human emotions and behavior. Neurotransmitters have specific roles in regulating mood and in determining behavioral, cognitive, and other physiological functions.

The Bio-Psychosocial Model of Stress

According to the Bio-Psychosocial Model, stress involves three components: an external component, an internal component, and the interaction between the external and internal components.

The external component involves environmental events that elicit a stress response. The stress response results from encounters with stimuli that are either physiologically or emotionally threatening and that disrupt the body's homeostasis. When we feel conflicted, frustrated, or pressured, we are usually aware of the presence of stressors. The most common stressors fall into four broad categories: personal, social/familial, work, and the environment.

It is an established scientific fact that stress has been linked to a variety of psychological and physical ailments. For example, bereavement can result in lowered immune system functioning. Stress is also related to the duration of the causative event. Acute stressors last for a relatively short duration and, because they are limited in time, are generally not considered to be a health risk. Chronic stressors are of relatively longer duration and can pose a serious health risk due to their prolonged activation of the body's stress response.

The internal component involves neurological and physiological reactions to stress. Hans Selye has identified three phases of stress:

- Alarm Reaction
- Stage of Resistance
- Exhaustion

This set of reactions mobilizes the body to deal with an impending threat. The Alarm Reaction is equivalent to the "fight-or-flight response." When a threat is perceived, the hypothalamus signals both the sympathetic nervous system and the pituitary gland. The sympathetic nervous system stimulates the adrenal glands, which then release corticosteroids to increase metabolism. This provides immediate energy for the body to respond. The pituitary gland releases adrenocorticotrophic hormone (ACTH), which also affects the adrenal glands. The adrenal glands then release epinephrine and norepinephrine, which prolong the fight-or-flight response. The Stage of Resistance is a continued state of arousal. If the stressful situation is prolonged, the high level of hormones released during the resistance phase may upset homeostasis and harm internal organs, leaving the organism vulnerable to disease. The Exhaustion stage occurs after prolonged resistance. During this stage, the body's energy reserves are finally exhausted.

When the state of stress is prolonged or intense, illness and disease can result, including headaches, insomnia, high blood pressure, gastrointestinal problems, skin disease, cardiovascular disease, kidney disease, and others.

Physical pain complicates this emotional situation. Pain, especially chronic pain, can create or exacerbate stress, depression, and anxiety. Pain patients who are treated in traditional ways often view their depression and anxiety as a stigma. They have been taught to view their emotional reactions as a sign of weakness, a "cop out," rather than as a very real condition with biological foundations. The "Martyr Syndrome" prevails, in some societies more than in others, where people who voice concerns about their pain are seen as complainers. Because of a lack of appropriate knowledge about various types of pain and associated stress on the part of medical professionals, pain patients end up taking a double hit—their spiral of suffering becomes more deeply entrenched, due to a pessimistic philosophy spouted indiscriminately by so-called professionals: "You will have to endure pain for rest of your life. Not a whole lot I can do."

Pain has a direct impact on how we experience our emotions. We know from the Bio-Psychosocial Model that treating the mind is as important as treating the body. We need emotional as well as physical safety in order to achieve equilibrium and get rid of pain. Ajrawat Air-Pulse Autonomic Therapy can help us achieve that goal.

How Ajrawat Air-Pulse Autonomic
Therapy Restores Homeostasis

In 1996, I introduced Ajrawat Air-Pulse Autonomic Therapy to my patients and made it a regular part of my dynamic model. I consider this to be a revolutionary advance in my treatment process, capable of healing the division between body and mind, and between conscious and unconscious bodily processes, in a way that promotes true recovery and healing from chronic pain, pain associated with stress, and stress itself.

Now that I have described the scientific basis for this therapy, it is time to describe how you can practice it, either by yourself or as part of a pain treatment plan.

How to Practice Ajrawat
Air-Pulse Autonomic Therapy

Position and Posture

Ajrawat Air-Pulse Autonomic Therapy can be done lying down, sitting up, in a semi-recumbent position, or in the fetal position. No particular posture is essential. However, the best position or posture is a semi-recumbent one, popularly known as the Khalistani Posture (a physiological, relaxed, free, self-determined, and sovereign posture). You sit in a comfortable, ergonomically, and physiologically correct posture, as one would sit in a recliner chair. Wear comfortable clothes. The environment should be quiet, with dimmed lights.

Air-Pulse Autonomic Meditation Technique

Position the palm of the right hand over the dorsal surface of the left hand, tightly snuggled. Then position the right thumb lengthwise over the pulsating left radial artery, which is positioned approximately half an inch below the base of left thumb on the volar side. The pressure applied by the thumb over the radial artery should be moderate. (An amputee can choose an alternate site on the other side of the body, such as the brachial artery, axillary artery, posterior tibial, or others.) After positioning your right thumb on the left radial artery, gently place your hands in your lap.

Sometimes, due to stress, you may encounter difficulty feeling the pulsation, but do not be disheartened. In that situation position your thumb over the approximate location of the artery and start the autonomic therapy. Most individuals will feel the pulse in a very short time, as autonomic therapy begins to take effect. It might take you a few times to feel the pulse in its full form. This is commonly seen in people who are chronically stressed, who have bent their wrists at an acute angle, or if their wrists are hyperextended.

After positioning your thumb on the radial pulse, close your eyes and start breathing gently through the nose, while focusing on the pulse and your navel. With each inhalation, push the navel out, and after each exhalation count to one silently. During each inhalation and exhalation, remain focused on the pulse and navel and continue to count your breaths. You breathe in and out five times. On the fifth exhalation smile with your mouth closed. Repeat this five-breath cycle for 15 to 20 minutes.

When you first start, you may find it hard to do this meditation therapy for more than a few minutes. But with practice and discipline, it is very easy to perform. In a very short time, usually less than a minute or two, you will feel your pulse rate and amplitude (or strength) both decrease. This indicates that your heart rate is slowing down, which lowers your blood pressure. It is this subtle yet effective activation of the heart and cardiovascular system that makes this meditation therapy perhaps the greatest medical discovery in human history. It dispels the generally held medical conviction that involuntary or autonomic functions of the body, such as breathing and heart rate, cannot be altered at will. Ajrawat Air-Pulse Autonomic Therapy will enlighten all of mankind to the new reality that one can indeed mobilize one's autonomic functions to help and heal body and mind.

By closing the eyes, breathing normally through the nose with the mouth closed, using Air-Pulse Navel Breathing (i.e., focusing on the navel while pushing the diaphragm out when taking a deep breath, the physiologically correct method of breathing), simultaneously pressing the left radial artery with the right thumb placed lengthwise over the pulse, and applying moderate pressure, you create a milieu to generate Dr. Ajrawat's Air-Pulse Homeostatic Reflex. It is this reflex which initiates the restoration of lost homeostasis, both mentally and physically.

Touching the Pulse

The sense of touch and pressure against the arterial pulse generates action potential in the peripheral nervous system via the mechanoreceptors and nerve fibers, thus mobilizing the calming and healing powers of the PNS as described before.

Air-Pulse Navel Breathing

Focusing the mind on the body's navel facilitates the process of deep abdominal breathing, increases the ability of the lungs to expand, improves oxygenation of the blood, increases tidal volume and lung capacity, and activates respiratory and parasympathetic nervous system activity.

With navel breathing, oxygenation of the blood and afferent mechanisms improves, which in turn causes stimulation of the parasympathetic nervous system, leading to bronchodilation and vasodilation, which further leads to improved circulation throughout the body. The end result is Autonomic Healing.

Smiling

Smiling stimulates the cranial nerves and, in turn, the parasympathetic nervous system. The smile component activates the facial nerve, and the air-pulse maneuver activates the vagus nerve, which in turn relaxes the facial and throat muscles, leading in turn to the activation of parasympathetic nervous system, which contributes to the restoration of lost homeostasis.

Closed Eyes

Keeping the eyes closed blocks any visual stimulation and prevents activation of various parts of the brain not conducive to relaxation and activating the parasympathetic nervous system. The goal is to prevent any unnecessary sensory input to the frontal and other parts of the brain, which minimizes the production of theta waves and hence improves the overall effectiveness of meditation therapy and relaxation.

Quiet Environment

Meditating in a quiet environment blocks any auditory stimulation, hence minimizing stimulation of the sympathetic nervous system and selectively activating the parasympathetic nervous system

Ajrawat Air-Pulse Maneuver for Relaxation

The Air-Pulse Maneuver is used during the early stages of meditation therapy. The patient, with eyes closed, holds the breath for few seconds and simultaneously presses harder on the left radial pulse with the right thumb for a similar duration (approximately five to seven seconds). This leads to instant relaxation, which is further accentuated and maintained by ongoing meditation therapy. It can be repeated if necessary during the meditation therapy session.

The Scientific Basis for Ajrawat Air-Pulse
Autonomic Therapy:
Bi-directional Psychosomatic Autonomic Feedback

Ajrawat Air-Pulse Autonomic Therapy utilizes the body's natural resources and mechanisms to restore homeostasis that has been lost due to pain, stress, physical or psychological trauma, hereditary causes, or disease.

The source of my invention was my knowledge and understanding of the concept of nociception, i.e., how tissue damage in the peripheral nervous system can generate painful impulses into the brain and the central nervous system. When an injury occurs to your body (such as blunt trauma or breaking of the skin, known as sharp trauma), special pain receptors called nociceptors are activated. Instantaneously, the nociceptors fire off a response—an impulse that heads through the nerve, into spinal cord, and all the way to the brain.

Unlike acute pain, chronic pain does not go away, often lasting for months or years. That's because pain receptors continue to send pain messages to the brain. Nociceptors can continue to send brain signals even in the absence of tissue damage. You continue to feel pain, even though there may no longer be a physically diagnosable cause of pain. Phantom limb pain and the pain of trigeminal neuralgia are two such examples.

I realized that constant stimulus (subtle and non noxious) of peripheral receptors and nerve endings could generate a stimulus to activate the parasympathetic system, thus leading to relaxation of the body and other therapeutic effects. Ajrawat Air-Pulse Autonomic Therapy is based on my concept of Bi-directional Psychosomatic Autonomic Feedback. What this means, in simple terms, is that a stimulus to the body leads to a perception and a response. In this case, Autonomic Therapy stimulates the central nervous system, the cardiovascular system, the respiratory system, and other systems of the body.

The constant stimulus by radial pulsation of the mechanoreceptors and pain receptors, which are found in abundance under the skin of the fingers, leads to the production of afferent impulses (impulses traveling from the outer parts of the body to the brain) via the process of depolarization of the nerves, which in turn activates and transmits electrical impulses.

These impulses reach the dorsal horn of the spinal cord, and finally reach the baroreceptors in the carotid sinuses and aortic arch, where activation of the vagal nerve takes place. These impulses, via the spinal cord, then reach the hypothalamus, cerebral cortex, and other parts of the brain, including the amygdala. Communication between various parts of the brain takes place, as well as with various organs and organ systems of the body.

The activation of baro-receptors in turn activates the vagus nerve, which in turn leads to activation of the parasympathetic nervous system, the relaxation of blood vessels, an increase in circulation to various parts of the body, and a decrease in heart rate and blood pressure.

This concept views physical pressure on the pulse as a sensation that can generate action potential (another term for an electrical current or an afferent impulse), which in turn can activate the central and peripheral nervous systems. The pressure of the thumb on the radial artery and the pulsation of the radial artery become a constant stimulus for the mechano-receptors and pain receptors, including merkel cells and bodies, pacinian corpuscles, meisners corpuscles, and free nerve endings, which are found in abundance under the surface of the skin. The constant stimulus of the mechanoreceptors by radial pulsation leads to a production of action potential via the process of depolarization of sensory nerves, which in turn activates and transmits the electrical impulses through A delta and C fibres.

These impulses synapse in the dorsal horn of the spinal cord and finally reach the baroreceptors in the carotid sinuses and aortic arch, where activation of the vagal nerve takes place. Via the spinal cord, these impulses stimulate communication between the pre-frontal cortex, the limbic system, the amygdala, and other structures. The hypothalamus activates the pituitary and adrenal glands. The sympathetic and parasympathetic nervous systems are thus activated, as well as various neuroendocrine and autonomic structures, all leading to the restoration of lost homeostasis.

Because of its scientific design and application, Ajrawat Air-Pulse Autonomic Therapy leads to the following results:

- Instant relaxation
- Calmness of mind
- Decrease in pulse rate
- Relaxed breathing
- Decrease in blood pressure
- Total blocking of mental chatter
- Instant cessation or minimization of negative or traumatic thoughts
- Instant cessation of anxiety or panic attacks
- Increase in body and skin temperature
- Decrease in intensity of pain
- Increase in energy and focus

Its long-term effects are equally impressive:

- Improved focus
- Improvement in skin luster and texture (especially a glow on the face)
- Improved insight
- Improved sleep
- Disappearance of depression
- Help with ADHD, OCD, and memory loss
- Deconditioning of the mind from negative thoughts and patterns
- Decrease in self-destructive behaviors
- Improvement in emotions and behavior
- Improvement in self-esteem and self-confidence
- Help with irritable bowel syndrome
- Decrease in weight
- Improved function of gut, heart, and other viscera
- Decrease in blood sugar levels

In the next chapter, I will describe how I use Ajrawat Air-Pulse Autonomic Therapy as part of my Dynamic Model, a multi-modality approach to treating chronic physical pain.

Chapter 4

Treating Chronic Physical Pain:
A Dynamic, Multi-Modality Approach

Ajrawat Air-Pulse Autonomic Therapy has helped my patients deal with stress, anxiety, panic attacks, and depression. Patients suffering from these conditions can self-administer the therapy at any time or place, to achieve lasting therapeutic results.

But as a pain specialist, I also work with patients suffering from much more severe problems, such as chronic physical pain. These patients need the full range of treatments that I offer at my Washington Pain Management Center. In this chapter I will explain how I successfully treat patients with a multi-modality approach, of which Ajrawat Air-Pulse Autonomic Therapy is one part. Patients who have suffered from years of debilitating physical and emotional pain have made astounding progress under my treatment.

One such individual is Gary. A few years ago, his life couldn't have been better. He was a perfectly healthy 27-year-old who enjoyed sports, worked out at the gym, and pursued a very active social life in British Columbia, Canada. But on a fateful day in May, Gary's productive life came to a crashing halt.

Gary was on his way to a weekend getaway. With a backpack full of clothes in his left hand, he was running to meet some friends at a ferry terminal. Once aboard the ferry, he felt a sudden pain on the left side of his lower back. He thought nothing of it, started stretching, and forgot about it.

The next morning Gary's nightmare began. He couldn't get out of bed, walk, or move his left leg. The pain was so unbearable he had tears in his eyes. He decided to head back home, which took almost five hours by car and ferry. Gary was experiencing such painful spasms that he screamed whenever his body jerked. Once home he couldn't get out of his car and was rushed to the hospital. There he received morphine injections for pain and had some tests done.

CAT scans showed that he had a slipped disc that was obtruding. The slipped disc was pinching his nerves, which caused pain to shoot from his left buttock into his thigh, and down his leg to the ankle.

"It felt like someone was stabbing me all the way down my left side," Garry recalled. "I couldn't stand straight or walk on my own."

His family doctor prescribed painkillers, such as oxycontin, oxycodone, and percocets, among many others. These pills temporarily reduced the pain, but didn't fix the problem. Gary tried many different healthcare providers, including chiropractors, acupuncturists, physiotherapists, and massage therapists, and none of them helped.

Gary's life took a complete nosedive. His personality and behavior changed. He became grouchy. He was always mad and yelling at those he loved. He didn't talk to his family and isolated himself from friends. He couldn't do the things he used to love most, like playing sports, working out, or just going out and having a good time.

Even his career was now on the line. He couldn't find a new job because he wasn't able to pass the physical testing requirements at various agencies. To make matters worse, he was fired from his current job because of too many missed days due to his back injury.

Pain had completely overtaken and ruined Gary's life. He was resigned to living in a nightmare.

"I became depressed because I had lost hope," he remembered. "I got used to the idea that I would have to spend the rest of my life that way. I started drinking heavily."

The Challenge of the Chronic Physical Pain

Chronic physical pain is a common health problem that afflicts one third to one half of people in the United States and around the world at any given time. It is one of the major causes of mental and physical disability, yet is commonly misdiagnosed and inappropriately treated. Sometimes it even goes completely undiagnosed.

As explained in the first chapter, science teaches us that various parts of the body and mind communicate with each other at multiple levels, starting from the smallest units, called cells, to larger units, such as tissues, organs, and organ systems. The Bio-Psychosocial Model acknowledges that mind and body not only communicate with each other, but also with the larger environment, including one's family, society, and culture. Through these multiple levels of communication, each system communicates with many other systems in various ways, and systems have the ability to affect each other through mutual feedback. Changes in one system of the body can affect all other systems. Therefore, treating one part or system of the body in isolation from others will not lead to pain relief, and often exacerbates it.

Gary's story shows why traditional approaches to chronic pain management are often not effective or even make the problem worse. He needed help in an integrated, systematic way, but the extent of his problems was greater than traditional medicine's ability to treat them. Acute and chronic pain has a profound affect on the mind and body. The lives of chronic pain sufferers change so profoundly that they can no longer cope with everyday life. Depression, irritability, loss of sleep, isolation, and lack of activity made Gary's life an endless misery. Trying (and failing) to escape this cycle of pain became the center of his life. Like many chronic pain patients, he became trapped on a never-ending merry-go-round of doctor shopping, excess medication, drug dependence, and surgery in his search for pain relief.

Perhaps you too are caught up in the same cycle of agonizing pain, excessive medication, and sleepless nights. Perhaps you too are physically and emotionally distressed, with your life brought to a standstill. Perhaps you have undergone multiple treatments, only to be told that your pain is unreal or all in your head, leaving you feeling bitter and disenfranchised.

If you recognize yourself in these descriptions, true relief is at hand. As a qualified pain specialist and a pioneer in the field of pain medicine and pain management, I have developed a new frame of reference to evaluate and treat chronic physical pain that is far superior to traditional ways of understanding and treating it.

Even though chronic physical pain is complex and multidimensional, most doctors continue to treat it in a one-dimensional manner, focusing on only part of the problem. Specialties like neurology, physical medicine and rehabilitation, anesthesiology, orthopedic surgery, and neurosurgery, when used in isolation from each other and with little understanding of the mind/body connection, often cause the sufferer more pain rather than solving the problem. Iatrogenic morbidity and pain (disability and pain resulting from either excessive or adjunctive treatments) is the major cause of chronic pain and disability in the United States. Gary received many different kinds of treatments from many different professionals, yet nothing helped. Why didn't he get better?

When interventions are not coordinated and holistic, when they don't take into consideration the unity of mind and body and the need to treat both simultaneously, such treatments do not bring healing to underlying pathology. A family physician prescribes drugs, a physical therapist provides therapy, a chiropractor manipulates the body. Yet these approaches often don't work because symptoms are being treated in an adjunctive manner, haphazardly and in isolation from each other. When health care providers and physicians treat a multidimensional problem in one-dimensional ways, by operating in isolation from each other, the cycle of pain and disability not only continues unbroken, but also can get worse. Pain sufferers become disabled and depressed, experiencing more pain in the process and becoming dependent or addicted to medication.

As the cycle of pain worsens, traditional medicine uses excessive, unnecessary, and often invasive procedures. Then, if the pain cannot be located in something obvious, such as a broken bone, torn ligament, or herniated disc, the traditional physician may decide that the pain is "unreal." This is not only incorrect, but also very insulting and demeaning to the pain patient's sense of self-respect and integrity. The patient has put his or her trust in the health care professional to attain pain relief, only to be misunderstood and neglected. This is not only unproductive in relieving pain, but makes the problem worse.

This is what happened to Gary. He lost his job, was isolated from family and friends, and couldn't enjoy the simplest of daily activities. His personality changed. He was angry and depressed. Any kind of trauma, whether it be physical, chemical, or psychological, can result in illness affecting both mind and body. Treating aspects of Gary's pain in isolation rather than in a comprehensive way creates a vicious cycle that becomes difficult to break, largely because physicians do not see how body and mind affect each other and are interrelated.

Another good example of why the complexity of pain demands new approaches is myofascial pain, which is produced by stress or damage to muscle tissue and fascia (the thin layer of connective tissue that supports and connects the muscles). Myofascial pain is often overlooked, yet it is the major cause of pain and dysfunction in the body. The muscles and fascia suffer the most wear and tear, but most health care professionals tend to focus on bones, discs, or nerves. Quite often, x-rays, scans, and other diagnostics do not detect the causes of myofascial pain, leading to the faulty conclusion that the pain "is all in the patient's head." Since the patient knows that the pain is real and not in any way imaginary, and continues to suffer in the worst possible way, the result is a chronic downward spiral of anger, depression, and, at times, even suicide.

Myofascial trigger points, which refer pain to the knees, elbows, wrists, and other joints, are often misdiagnosed as rheumatoid arthritis, and patients are then started on a regimen of cytotoxic drugs, such as methotrexate and oral steroids, which can lead to serious side effects and damage to the body. This often is the case when specialists (such as rheumatologists) are used to treating one particular type of diagnosis with one particular or uni-dimensional approach, without being innovative or aware of different possibilities for diagnosis and multimodality treatments. The result, especially in the field of rheumatology, is chronic pain and disability.

It is no longer scientific to ignore the psychosocial components of pain, while attempting to label a patient's pain as "unreal." Effective pain treatment recognizes that the problem of pain is complex and multidimensional. The physician must evaluate not just bodily factors, diagnostics (like x-rays or scans), or psychological factors, but all factors, in combination, that are involved in producing pain.

Accordingly, no one should be surprised that just as traumatic injury to the body can affect the mind and the person's social functioning, traumatic changes in the social environment can affect not only the mind, but also the body. Body and mind are one and completely interrelated. Had Gary never suffered a back injury, but had lost his job and been out of work for months, that emotional trauma would have been experienced physically in his body. In the same way, treating Gary's back pain was not just a question of identifying and treating the bodily source of that pain; rather, a comprehensive, holistic approach would help him deal with his anger, depression, lack of sleep, and deep sense of loss with regard to his family, friends, and career.

I have treated many patients in my practice who were psychologically happy and well adjusted prior to their physical trauma and pain. In a short time, these patients became anxious and depressed because of their persistent pain. I must also point out, however, that chronic depression or anxiety can not only lower one's natural pain threshold, but can in fact precipitate real pain, which in a majority of cases is myofascial in nature. This type of psychogenic pain is all too real to its sufferers.

Millions of individuals experiencing chronic physical pain needlessly suffer because they cannot find help that is appropriate to their multifaceted needs. I believe that every health problem, no matter how deep seated and complex, has a remedy and a solution. In order to treat pain effectively, one must be a specialist with appropriate fellowship training in pain management, where one is trained to understand and evaluate the various components involved in producing the pain. We all know that for any physician to be called a specialist, he or she must have appropriate post residency fellowship training, such as takes place in the fields of cardiology, endocrinology, gastroentrology, and others.

It was my frustration with existing therapies and a desire to aid those suffering, not only in this country but around the world, that led me to create my revolutionary new therapies. I've successfully used these therapies with patients over many years. I am now convinced we have the ability to scientifically conquer pain and make this a pain free world. The purpose of this book is to show how that goal can be achieved by healing the pain that affects you.

Understanding Human Neurochemistry:
How is Pain Experienced by the Body?

How does the brain distinguish between a pleasant sensation and a painful one? How does this information travel from the body to the brain, and then back into a reaction? Why do some forms of pain become chronic pain? And how does an understanding of these processes influence how I treat pain?

When something happens to the body or in our environment, the sensory nerves sends messages to the brain via the spinal cord. The brain sends information back to the motor nerves, which help us move our arms and legs and perform a whole range of actions. The nervous system is a complicated, two-way communication system. How does that communication system work in processing physical pain?

Let's say you're working on a carpentry project and you hit your thumb with the hammer. A sensory nerve in your peripheral nervous system responds to this event and produces a chemical response. If you brushed your thumb with a feather instead of hitting it with a hammer, the sensory nerve would have produced a different chemical response. These chemical responses determine how sensations are interpreted. A hammer blow causes nerves to send one type of signal, while a feather causes another type.

When an injury occurs to your body (such as blunt trauma, or breaking of the skin, known as sharp trauma), special pain receptors called nociceptors are activated. Instantaneously, the nociceptors fire off a response—an impulse that heads through the nerve, into spinal cord, and all the way to the brain. What's interesting is that even a potential injury (like an indentation in the skin, which compresses the tissues without breaking the skin) also activates the nociceptors. The damage to the affected tissue causes local inflammation, which in turn causes the liberation of pain producing substances like prostaglandins, bradykinin, kines and others. These substances sensitize the nerve endings and produce painful impulses that travel towards the brain, chemicals are released, which in turn sends an electrical charge along the spinal cord. This goes to the dorsal horn of the spinal cord, the part of the spine that receives afferent information. When the dorsal horn senses the electrical charges sent to it, more neurotransmitters are released. Pain then goes to the brain.

Many research scientists and physicians call the dorsal horn the "Pain Gate." Drs. Patrick Wall and Ronald Melzack, my fellow members and colleagues from IAPS (International Association for the

Study of Pain) were awarded the Nobel Prize for proposing their gate control theory of pain, which has been one of the prime models for understanding the process of nociception and modulation of pain.

In addition, the spinal cord makes some of its own decisions, called reflexes. The dorsal horn acts as an information hub, simultaneously directing impulses to the brain and back down the spinal cord to the area of injury. Your brain doesn't have to tell you to grab your thumb, because the dorsal horn has already sent that message.

Even though the spinal reflex takes place at the dorsal horn, the pain signal continues to the brain. Your problem is not over simply because there has been a stimulus (hitting your thumb with the hammer) and a response (grabbing your thumb). Your thumb still needs to be healed. In addition, your brain needs to make sense of what has happened. Pain gets catalogued in your brain's library, and emotions become associated with banging your thumb.

The thalamus is the part of the brain that receives the pain signal, which it then directs to different parts of the brain for interpretation. For example, the cortex figures out where the pain came from and compares it to other kinds of pain you have suffered before. Have you hit your thumb before? Was this pain worse? The thalamus also sends signals to the limbic system, which is the emotional center of the brain. With some pain you will cry, with other pain you will not. The limbic system decides. You associate feelings with every sensation in your body, and each feeling generates a response. After you hit you thumb with the hammer, your heart rate may increase, you may break out into a sweat, you may start breathing heavily.

What makes pain complicated is the interrelationship between these numerous systems in the body and mind. Pain is not just a two-way system of cause and effect: your physical and emotional response to pain is affected by numerous factors, such as your mood, your past experiences, your ethnicity, and your expectations, among others. These factors can change the way you interpret pain at any given time.

If you hit your thumb with a hammer right after your teenager talks back to you, you will have a different response than if you just received a big promotion at work. If your thumb became infected the last time you hit it with a hammer, your reaction will be different than if you quickly recovered the last time it happened. Your personal history and emotional response will determine how you respond to pain and how you recover from it.

We saw how Gary not only injured his back, but also lost his job and became isolated from family and friends as a result of his anger and depression. Any kind of trauma, whether it be physical, chemical, or psychological, can result in illness affecting both mind and body. In fact, there is a strong link between depression and chronic pain. And this is because pain is complex on both a physical and emotional level.

Understanding Nociceptive and Neuropathic Pain

As stated before, the Bio-Psychosocial Model is based on the premise that pain is an experience that cannot be seen as separate from the patient's mental state, environment, and cultural background. Whenever a patient comes to me complaining of pain, no matter where it is located and no matter how long its duration, it is critical that I investigate the mental and environmental factors contributing to it.

It's important to understand the differences between nociceptive and neuropathic pain, because these differences figure importantly in my pain treatment model.

Nociceptive Pain

When parts of the body suffer damage, nociceptors are the sensory receptors which sense and respond to that pain by signaling tissue irritation, impending injury, or actual injury. When activated, the nociceptors transmit pain signals via the peripheral nerves as well as the spinal cord to the brain. This type of pain is typically well localized in a particular part or area of the body, and often has an aching or throbbing quality. Visceral pain is a type of nociceptive pain that involves the internal organs. It tends to be episodic and poorly localized.

Nociceptive pain is usually time limited—when the tissue damage heals, the pain typically resolves. (Arthritic pain is a notable exception in that it is not time limited.). Examples of nociceptive pain include sprains, bone fractures, burns, bumps, bruises, inflammations, obstructions, and myofascial pain.

Neuropathic Pain

Neuropathic pain is the result of an injury or malfunction in the peripheral or central nervous system. The pain is often triggered by an injury, but this injury may or may not involve actual damage to the nervous system. Nerves can be compressed in many ways: by tumors, scar tissue, when entrapped by muscles or inflamed by infection, damaged by diabetes (high blood glucose), damaged by drugs used in chemotherapy, or from vitamin B deficiency. The pain frequently has a burning or electric shock quality. The pain may persist for months or years beyond the apparent healing of any damaged tissues. In this type of pain, the pain signals no longer represent an alarm about ongoing or impending injury; instead the alarm system itself is malfunctioning. This is why neuropathic pain is frequently chronic, and tends to have a less robust response to traditional treatment.

Examples include cancer pain, phantom limb pain, entrapment neuropathy (e.g., carpal tunnel syndrome, scalene syndrome), and peripheral neuropathy (widespread nerve damage). Diabetes is the most common cause of peripheral neuropathy, but the condition can also be caused by chronic alcohol use, exposure to other toxins (including many chemotherapies), vitamin deficiencies, and a large variety of other medical conditions.

In some conditions, pain appears to be caused by a complex mixture of nociceptive and neuropathic factors.

How Does Acute Pain Become Chronic Pain?

There are two forms of pain, acute and chronic. The most debilitating, by far, is chronic pain.

If you injure your thumb, it should heal over time and your pain will stop. This is called acute pain—the pain does not persist after the initial injury has healed because the nociceptors (the special pain receptors) no longer detect any tissue damage or potential injury.

In contrast, chronic pain does not go away after the initial injury heals, often lasting for months or years. That's because pain receptors continue to send pain messages to the brain. This can be caused by a disease or condition that continuously causes damage to the body.

For example, if you have pain in the knees, the general perception and diagnosis by health care professionals is that you have bony changes in your joints, called osteophyte formation, or you have loss of cartilage that causes pain in the joints. Knee pain is also often diagnosed as arthritis, but often the source of pain is not in the joint itself but in the myofascial trigger points, which transfer or refer pain to the joint. This phenomenon is called referred pain to a zone of reference. So, in other words, trigger points can be in the groin or mid-thigh area, which become tender to the touch, but the pain is felt inside of the knee, which is part of the zone of reference. If the pain exists for a certain duration of time, it is called chronic pain. It often becomes worse once the misguided decision is made to perform knee surgery or joint replacement—misguided, because the source of the pain isn't the knee, but an area near the knee. That is why it is so important to have a correct understanding of the sources of pain.

In chronic pain, nociceptors can continue to send pain signals to the brain even in the absence of tissue damage. You continue to feel pain, even though there may no longer be a physical cause for it. This complexity makes chronic pain difficult to diagnose and even more difficult to treat. It is the reason why many doctors, operating out of old models, dismiss their patients' complaints.

Healing Gary: A New Multidisciplinary Medical Paradigm

After two years of living in hell, Gary finally got his lucky break. He attended a conference in British Columbia and heard me speaking about my pain management techniques. He arranged for a consultation and flew to my Pain Management Center in Washington D.C. This was a turning point in his life. Gary had been let down by many medical experts in the past, but the first time I saw him, I already knew what ailed him.

As Gary recalled later: "Dr. Ajrawat blew my mind by looking at me and saying, 'Son, you have a disc problem in your back, and your left leg is longer than your right.' He said this just by looking me over for a few seconds."

I was confident that I could help Gary. My center employs specialists working in an interdisciplinary format that is based on the Bio-psychosocial Model of illness. With each patient, we use a multidisciplinary approach to treat the whole person. That means that Gary received a full range of somatic, cognitive, and behavioral therapies in an integrated treatment program tailored to his individual needs.

Since Gary's pain affected every aspect his life, I began by identifying all the factors that perpetuated and complemented his pain. Then I started a treatment program with trigger point injections, nerve blocks, physical rehabilitation, strengthening and stretching exercises, individual psychotherapy, medication therapy, autonomic meditation therapy, hot packs, electrical stimulation, antidepressants, and both narcotic and non-narcotic pain medication. I treated his sleep disturbance. I helped him regain his strength, flexibility, and endurance through a program of neuromuscular conditioning, physical rehabilitation, strengthening and stretching exercises, and correction of leg length inequality. Finally, the psychological parts of his problem had to be addressed. Gary's depression was alleviated and his cognition improved through meditation and my Air-Pulse Amygdala Therapy, while his stress and anxiety were treated with supportive psychotherapy.

Gary received state of the art medical treatments that he had never seen or experienced before, and every treatment made him feel better. Soon I had Gary running, bending, and doing things that he hadn't been able to do since his injury. After two weeks with me he was a new man. His pain left, his depression disappeared, and he was able to resume a normal life back in British Columbia. With my treatment, Gary's ability and agility have improved to the point where he now regularly runs track and is working full time.

M.V.: Back From Hell

The story of M.V. is another example of how my revolutionary, multidimensional therapies can help patients ease their suffering from chronic pain.

When he was 69, M.V. underwent a radical prostatectomy for cancer. Before the surgery he was in the best possible shape: stretching every morning and running four miles on a treadmill every other day. He felt and looked much younger than his age.

After the surgery, it was a different story. M.V. entered what was the worst period in his life. Two months after the procedure, he felt he had aged ten years. Despite a lot of painkillers, he was suffering. He had to go to the bathroom eight or ten times a night. His surgeon was lost, not knowing what was going on or what to prescribe, except for a routine pill for the bladder.

"I decided to see another urologist in my area, with a good rating, to get a second opinion and hopefully get some relief," M.V. recalled. "Perhaps I had another cancer somewhere? He ordered urine and blood tests, a CAT scan, and did a cystoscopy. He saw nothing wrong. Good news, he said—no infection, no cancer. But from there on, what to do?"

M.V.'s doctor, operating from the biomedical model, thought that the case was solved once he found no apparent cause for pain in his patient's body. This shows the limitations of traditional diagnostic techniques and treatments. One of M.V.'s legs was shorter than the other and that caused posture compensations and then cramps. He had pain moving from one part of the body to another, from his thighs to his back and shoulders, but no doctor found a way to treat him for this terrible condition.

"As soon as there was no flesh to cut," M.V. said, "I was no longer an interesting case, and the doctor rather rudely told me that he couldn't do anything for me. Move along—I have other patients waiting."

If urologists couldn't do anything for M.V., he had to find someone else to help alleviate his pain. He had heard about pain management, found me by surfing the web, and made an appointment.

"This first appointment was a pleasant surprise," M.V. recalled. "I was used to doctors that kept you only ten minutes the first time, and then three minutes in each following visit. With Dr. Ajrawat, the diagnostic took an hour and a half. He told me, 'It's an ethical choice—with my patients, I don't look at my watch.' I was already feeling better."

As with all patients, I used a multidimensional approach with M.V.: trigger point injections, nerve blocks, physical rehabilitation, Ajrawat Air-Pulse Autonomic Therapy, psychotherapy, strengthening and stretching exercises, and medication. Not surprisingly, this treatment takes time: three one-hour sessions a week for six or more weeks, depending on the case. But it leads to tangible results, and M.V. was not an exception.

"After one month of pain management, I discovered its first benefits," M.V. said. "My first benchmark was to recover the ability to sleep. Since week one of treatment, I slept without sleeping pills. The second benchmark was that the level of pain was clearly lower and I regained control of my bladder. For the first time in six months I didn't put on a diaper, but a pad.

"But there is another benefit to pain management," he continued. "I had felt ten years older, but now my body feels younger. The feeling of age is strongly related to body stiffness. Knowingly or not, when we grow older we let our bodies become less and less flexible. It's like an inside 'carapace' limiting our movements. Right now, thanks to pain management, I am shedding that carapace and going back in time."

D.B.: An End to Chronic Pain

D.B. hated completing pain assessments (on a scale of "1" to "10," how severe is your pain?) every time she sought treatment for her chronic back pain.

"One day as I sat in a doctor's office completing the pain assessment," she recalls, "I found my mind wandering. Three thoughts came to mind: (1) my life was becoming a living hell because the chronic back pain was not only controlling my body, but also interfering with my ability to lead a normal, productive, and active life; (2) none of the doctors I had visited so far was able to offer a proper diagnosis and treatment plan that would relieve the pain; and (3) I was beginning to accept the fact that I was never going to be pain free.

"No one can imagine what it is like to live in chronic pain unless you are a sufferer," D.B. says. "Dealing with pain every day is difficult, but losing the hope of ever being healed is more devastating.

When I left the doctor's office that day, I got in my car and began to cry. How could I accept this pain?"

D.B. had been experiencing varying degrees of pain for almost 10 years. In September 2006, she awoke from sleep in excruciating pain from a large muscle spasm that started above her left shoulder blade and radiated down her left arm to her fingertips. Her immediate thought was that she had slept in an awkward position and the pain would eventually go away.

Much to D.B.'s surprise, the pain continued to intensify and seemed out of proportion to what one would expect from a muscle spasm. After a few days of taking over-the-counter pain medication, she scheduled an appointment with her primary care physician. After an exam, the doctor recommended she have an MRI, schedule an appointment with a pain specialist, and consider physical therapy. D.B. was also to continue taking Motrin.

The pain specialist reviewed the MRI results and told D.B. she had four herniated discs. He recommended she take physical therapy three times a week for six weeks. He also prescribed Motrin (800 mg.), Neurontin (600 mg.), and Zanaflex (4 mg.). These medications made her extremely drowsy. While D.B. was able to sleep, the pain did not improve.

The physical therapy lasted five months instead of the initial six weeks, but still there was no improvement. D.B.'s mental state was deteriorating.

"Finally, he recommended that I take a morphine pack as a last resort," D.B. recalls. "If this didn't work, he recommended that I consider back surgery. Because of the horror stories that I had heard about people who had back surgery, I did not consider it to be an option. I returned to my primary care physician. She suggested that I take nerve tests for carpel tunnel syndrome. She also referred me to a spine treatment center. On the very first visit, the doctor reviewed my MRI and stated that there was nothing that he could do for me except recommend surgery. I left the doctor's office feeling depressed and deflated. All this time had elapsed, and none of the doctors had offered a treatment plan that yielded results."

In December 2007, D.B. felt a tingling pain down her left thigh. After a visit with her primary care physician she was referred to a neurologist, who told her she was experiencing nerve pain. The doctor kept D.B. on the same medications—Motrin, Neurontin, and Zanaflex—but added Tramadol and Cymbalta for pain.

"This doctor indicated that chronic pain can sometimes be a psychosomatic condition. The physical problem exists, but psychological factors play a role in determining the person's experience of that problem. Feelings of depression or frustration can actually make the pain worse. Cymbalta, a drug used for depression, was added to trick my brain into believing that I was not in pain. Eventually I became an insomniac and the neurologist added Ambien CR to help me sleep. Eventually I stopped seeing this doctor. I was simply taking too many drugs and was worried about the side effects."

In October 2008, D.B. set out to find a new doctor and found my practice on the internet.

"From the moment that I met Dr. Ajrawat," D.B. recalls, "I knew that I would not leave the Washington Pain Management Center the same way that I entered. I had been in constant pain since September 2006. I was taking multiple medications. I could barely straighten my back. I planned to travel to Egypt in April 2009, but knew I wouldn't be able to do so in my current state. Dr. Ajrawat assured me that I would be able to make the trip.

"On my initial visit, Dr. Ajrawat conducted a thorough consultation and evaluation. He outlined a plan that he asserted would give me immediate relief. I left that first visit feeling confident that Dr. Ajrawat would offer a personalized treatment plan that would, over time, improve my quality of life. I was looking forward to the journey.

"I started visiting Dr. Ajrawat three times a week, starting in November 2008. I was treated with multi-modality treatments, which included nerve blocks, trigger point injections, physical rehabilitation, meditation therapy, strengthening and stretching exercises, hot packs, and electrical stimulation. Within three weeks I was completely off all the medications I had been taking when I started with Dr. Ajrawat and I began to feel relief from my pain. As the weeks went by, not only was I better physically, but mentally as well. I returned to my regular routines and activities. I was even able to walk two miles, three times a week.

"In April 2009—just five months after I started at Washington Pain Management Center—Dr. Ajrawat had me ready for my trip to Egypt. It was a trip of a lifetime, made possible by his wonderful treatment. I was pain free and didn't experience any problems on the 10-day trip. He provided me with instructions for the long flight—take an aisle seat and stretch every couple of hours.

"When I arrived in Cairo I was ecstatic. Over the next nine days I climbed the pyramids, road a camel twice, drove a four-wheel quad through the Sahara desert to a Bedouin village, and walked through all the historical sites from Cairo to Aswan.

"Now I visit the Washington Pain Management Center once a week. While I occasionally take Tylenol or Advil, I remain off any prescription medications.

"I am so thankful to Dr. Ajrawat. He works tirelessly to ease the pain and suffering of his patients. He offers the hope of healing to countless people every day. When I think of him, the following quote comes to mind:

The good physician treats the disease; the great physician treats the patient who has the disease.

Dr. William Osler, 1849-1919

"I am blessed to have found Dr. Ajrawat and highly recommend his treatment plan to any pain sufferer."

Lori: From a Cocoon to a Budding Flower

Lori is yet another example of how traditional medical approaches not only fail to provide relief to pain sufferers, but often fail to correctly diagnose the problem.

Lori's ordeal began after she was involved in a car accident. She suffered whiplash, a torn muscle extending from her shoulder to her neck, and a concussion. She began to suffer from excruciating headaches that incapacitated her on a daily basis. She experienced a burning sensation in the middle of her back and an aching, pulsing pain along the right side of her head.

"The pain made it hard for me to think or concentrate," Lori recalled. "My vision was affected with extreme photosensitivity. My hearing was also affected, to the point that a mere whisper sounded like someone yelling. I experienced nausea and vomiting, and had to lie down in a quiet, dark room to deal with my symptoms. I suffered frequent memory lapses and sometimes went whole days remembering only fragments of things that had happened to me. My speech was slurred and my equilibrium became impaired."

Lori, who is a registered nurse by profession, consulted three neurologists, who each gave conflicting diagnoses. Her primary care physicians could only prescribe pain medication. Psychologists attributed her problems to a range of childhood issues, from the effects of molestation to a diagnosis of dissociative personality disorder. She received numerous kinds of medication, including Maxalt, Imitrex, Daypro, Topamax, Neurontin, Elavil, DHE, Tylenol # 3, and Toradol. None of them provided sustained relief. Nor did botox injections and acupuncture.

"I was accused of 'doctor shopping' as I sought professional care to deal with my daily headaches," Lori said. "I was accused of being drug impaired and drug addicted. My family wanted me to go to rehab. I had to set up family meetings with doctors to explain to my children and former husband that I was not abusing my medication. I was terminated from a job that I adored because of my physical problems."

While sitting in a doctor's office one day and leafing through magazines, Lori came across my pain center and treatment modalities.

"Dr. Ajrawat, his wife, and his staff have been a godsend to me," Lori said. "I have found a doctor with a sincere desire to help, a listening ear, and much needed empathy.

"During my first visit, I was feeling extremely emotional and depressed and just wanted to run away. But after receiving trigger point injections and nerve blocks, learning Dr. Ajrawat's meditation therapy, and incorporating exercise and a better diet into my life, I feel like a new person. As I said to Dr. Ajrawat, 'Before I felt like I was in a cocoon, now I feel like a budding flower.'

"I recently visited my family in Maine. They were surprised to see the glow on my face. They apologized for accusing me of being addicted to medicine, because my speech had been slurred in the past due to my pain. Now I feel so much better, emotionally and physically. I am back to being myself again and have returned to my old job as a full time nursing supervisor.

"I have stopped all my pain medications, have a more positive outlook on life, and am slowly returning to my original self," Lori concluded. "I thank God for my new husband who has stood beside me through all this and lifted me up when I was down. My friends all tell me I speak differently and seem happy. I still on occasion have a headache, but I can truly, honestly say that my life has been saved by Dr. Ajrawat's approaches to treating the whole person."

Laura: Back from the Brink

At age 31, Laura was in a severe automobile accident that changed her life. She was ejected from her vehicle, skidded across the pavement, and landed under an 18-wheeler tractor-trailer. Her left knee was pinned by two of the truck's wheels.

Miraculously, no bones were broken; however, Laura suffered severe second and third degree burns from abrasion against the pavement, which covered two-thirds of her left leg. After undergoing numerous skin grafts over the course of eight months, she was then referred to the Washington Pain Medicine Center.

I treated Laura with sympathetic nerve blocks, trigger point injections, physical therapy, strengthening and stretching exercises, and pain medication. She also participated in individual and group psychotherapy with my wife and associate Dr. Sukhveen Kaur Ajrawat, the staff psychiatrist especially trained in the psychological and psychiatric aspects of pain and stress. In addition, Laura learned air-pulse meditation therapy.

"The care I received at the Washington Pain Medicine Center allowed me to return to work within two months after beginning my treatment," says Laura, who is a registered nurse practitioner. "Nowadays, it is rare to find a doctor who sincerely cares about his patients' emotional and physical well-being. For me, it has been a blessing beyond words to have a doctor who has always put my needs first, and who does what is best for me to achieve and maintain my optimal health. To see these actions faithfully carried out on a daily basis year after year conveys that this is a physician who truly cares about you as a person and not just as a patient. My faith in God has helped to guide and strengthen me throughout this trial, and one of many blessings I have received along the way is Dr. Ajrawat and his team."

The pain suffered by Gary, M.V., D.B., Lori, and Laura is not unusual. And thanks to the therapies I have developed and that are readily available to you, it is also not unusual for chronic pain sufferers like these to find relief and regain their lives. I believe there is a cure for every type of pain, no matter how severe and chronic, and this book will show how my proven treatments can help you and your loved ones regain their health and well-being, and live pain-free lives.

Treating pain has been the passion of my life. I am no less committed to this battle than a warrior fighting a physical battle. The only difference is that pain treatment requires unrelenting persistence, constant enthusiasm, boundless patience, and the patient's cooperation and compliance. I do not engage in battles that I am not going to win, and winning the battle against pain will always be my true professional passion.

In fact, after 25 years of practice, my enthusiasm is not only unaltered, but also stronger than ever. Assisted by my wife, Dr. Sukhveen Kaur Ajrawat, a board certified psychiatrist with specialized training in the psychological and psychiatric aspects of pain and stress, my journey in this field has been immensely rewarding. Our sincere efforts have helped us earn the blessings of our patients, the best reward one can ask for.

And yet, even with more holistic and less invasive methods of treating pain, and a greater acceptance of the mind/body connection in healing and recovery, my chronic pain patients all too frequently ask me the same question: "Doctor, how come you spent so much time getting to know my medical history, when other doctors rushed me out of their offices in less than five minutes? How come you believed everything I said, while the others made me feel like I was crazy?"

My answer is often the same to each patient: "First, I am a pain specialist by training. Second, it is my job to figure out the cause of your pain and help you in the best ways that I possibly can."

Such kind words only make me more humble in my commitment to solve this colossal problem confronting all of humanity.

Eight Core Therapeutic Practices

In my Dynamic Model, pain patients can take advantage of various options to correct faulty frames of reference imposed on them by unaware professionals. The patient is educated about all aspects of their diagnosis and treatment options. The patient is encouraged to ask questions and share any concerns he or she might have. I avoid being dogmatic about any of the various approaches I advise. Dogma gets in the way of helping sufferers. Nor do I chase after fads or distort the truth.

The main goal of my dynamic model is to help individuals develop a healthy mind and body, leading to the complete empowerment of one's self. To live in this world with dignity and self-respect, one must have that balance. The secret to the positive outcomes of my patients has been simply this: individuals suffering from chronic pain receive one-on-one quality care that is tailored appropriately to their specific needs.

My pain management model is based on eight core therapeutic practices. Later on I will explain in greater detail how my methods work, but here is an overview:

1) Utilization of the specialized and interdisciplinary Bio-Psychosocial Model.

I've described how I treat each patient in a holistic way, viewing body and mind as inseparable, interrelated entities, as I work to heal *all* causes of pain affecting each individual I encounter.

2) Careful and concrete diagnosis based on getting a detailed history of the patient, a thorough physical exam, a psychological evaluation, and x rays, scans, and blood work when necessary.

Too often, inaccurate diagnosis only adds to a patient's woes. I emphasize the importance of an accurate, comprehensive diagnosis as the first step in promoting lasting pain relief.

I firmly believe that a thorough understanding of the patient's history and a comprehensive physical exam pertinent to the symptoms of pain, especially with special reference to myofascial pain and others, is absolutely essential to make a correct diagnosis

3)   Utilization of Dr. Ajrawat's Dynamic Model for Management of Pain.

In an outpatient pain center, under one roof, my team provides a range of multimodality treatments, including nerve blocks, trigger point injections, facet joint blocks, SI joint blocks, physical rehabilitation, strengthening and stretching exercises, walking alternated with jogging, adjunctive treatments like hot packs, electrical stimulation, psychotherapy (individual, family, and group), and pharmacotherapy (use of both narcotic and non-narcotic analgesics, antidepressants, and other drugs).   The centerpiece of my treatment is Ajrawat Air-Pulse Autonomic Therapy.

Whenever necessary, the services of various specialty consultants are utilized. Diagnostic testing, such as x rays, scans (MRI, CT scans, EMG), blood work, and others, are generally utilized as additional and secondary criteria and not as primary criteria to diagnose pain.

4) Stringent and discretionary use of pharmaco-therapeutic modalities (or drugs), particularly narcotic analgesics. Keeping the patient disciplined and informed, through education about drug dependence and addiction.

I adhere to very firm, disciplined, and stringent criteria in prescribing pain medication to patients, especially when it comes to narcotic analgesics. I educate and motivate my patients to avoid using excess or unnecessary medication, but without compromising the quality of their care.

Patients are advised to use medication on a time-contingent basis and to use the least amounts possible to prevent drug dependence or addiction. Prescriptions, especially narcotic analgesics, are given in very small dosages and on a weekly basis to prevent abuse. Patients are cautioned against polypharmacy (taking more medication than is actually needed and seeking medication from multiple sources). The use of cytotoxic and anticancer drugs, such as methotrexate, and other categories of drugs, like botox, are deferred for the treatment of non-malignant pain.

Very stringent criteria are followed when using oral, intra-articular, or epidural steroids. Excessive use of these agents can lead to systemic side effects and structural defects, like Cushing's syndrome (damage to adrenal glands) and boggy joints.

A combination of antidepressant medications, especially tricyclic, doxepin, trazadone, and others, are used to enhance the patient's sleep, rather than tranquilizers, sedatives, hypnotics, or other depressant and habit forming medications.

The use of drugs like methadone to treat pain is outright wrong and should not be condoned by any professional. Drugs like ketamine and propofol, when used by overzealous physicians without proper training, knowledge, and skill, has led to serious complications and the deaths of some famous people. These drugs are meant to be used only during the induction of general anesthesia and not for pain management. Unfortunately, many people confuse pain management with the field of anesthesiology. Most anesthesiologists do not have formal training in pain management. They lack formal training and appropriate peer review by qualified (fellowship trained) pain specialists. Other disciplines, such as neurology, physical medicine, and rehabilitation, though understood to be alternative specialties for pain management, have their own respective limitations in providing full care. The public and medical professions await the development of pain management as a full-fledged medical specialty and the readily available services of qualified pain specialists.

5) Enthusiasm, empathy, and open-ended communication in dealing with patients, including patient education.

My wife and I work closely with each patient, forming close bonds and emphasizing the necessity of listening carefully to their concerns.

This helps alleviate the patient's uncertainty about his or her disorder, which in turn has its own therapeutic value because it puts the patient at ease.

6) A positive therapeutic alliance between myself and the patient, and a deep engagement with the patient's treatment plan. Keeping the patient motivated and actively engaged in the pain center and home setting is very important to achieve the desired therapeutic goals.

Chronic pain patients who have become unwilling participants in a never-ending merry-go-round in search for pain relief need discipline, motivation, and positive reinforcement. I encourage my patients to follow the treatment regimens at the pain center strictly, to be active participants in their treatment plan, and to participate diligently in returning to a pre-pain functional level, in order to feel mentally and physically healthy and self-empowered once again.

As a qualified pain specialist, I firmly believe that patients are inherently motivated to keep their appointments because of their desire to achieve pain relief and to restore their lost functionality. However, this becomes a great challenge when treating workers compensation or car accident cases.

I am an advocate of best patient care as well as patients' appropriate financial compensation in work related injury cases. However, because of the complexities of the American workers compensation system, when lawyers get involved in these kinds of cases conflicts of interest often develop between my goals as a doctor and the financial interests of third parties; thus, treatment often gets disrupted. As a result, because of unnecessary interventions, excessive adjunctive methods, and compensation issues, patients often end up going down the declining path of permanent disability, pain, and stress. A life that could have been restored to its normalcy becomes permanently disabled.

The "disability syndrome" has become a major problem in the United States, causing the nation billions of dollars in disability payments, lawyers' fees, and compensation. Aside from the pain this causes patients, it puts an unfair and unnecessary burden on the taxpayer.

7) The prevention of unnecessary diagnostic, medical, and surgical interventions and referrals. The use of various so-called advanced pain management techniques, such as morphine pumps, radiofrequency ablation, and the insertion of dorsal column or neuro-stimulators and joint replacements, is deferred, as they often lead to more chronicity, complications, and iatrogenic morbidity.

My holistic, multi-modality approach, emphasizing accuracy of diagnosis and treatment, prevents patients from wasting their time and money on unneeded procedures. This lessens the occurrence of iatrogenic morbidity and pain, one of the major causes of pain and disability in the United States. Conservative and effective methods of pain management should be the top priority. Physicians must affirm and practice the Hippocratic Oath, "Do no harm." Keeping an open mind without being dogmatic can be very helpful in accomplishing the desired therapeutic goals.

8) A carefully planned schedule of follow-up treatments.

After the patient has achieved complete or significant relief from pain, he or she is often discharged from active care. When discharged from my direct care, patients are advised to keep their daily schedule of strengthening and stretching exercises, alternating walking with jogging, diet regulation, and daily practice of Ajrawat Air-Pulse Autonomic Therapy. They are also advised to return for immediate treatment should any serious reoccurrence of their pain take place.

How My Multimodality Treatments Work

Here I describe in detail my individual treatments.

Nerve blocks

Nerve blocks are an important part of my multimodality approach to treating pain. A nerve block is an anesthetic or anti-inflammatory injection targeted toward a certain nerve or group of nerves. The purpose of the injection is to "turn off" a pain signal or break the cycle of pain coming from a specific location in the body or to decrease inflammation in that area.

In addition to interrupting the painful impulse, or nociceptive input, the anesthetic also helps relieve muscle spasms associated with certain painful disorders, such as myofascial pain disorder or fibromyalgia. Nerve blocks can interrupt the spinal reflex that is often responsible for producing and maintaining pain. They can block sympathetic fibers, leading to the interruption and reduction of sympathetic hyperactivity and improvement of circulation and relief of pain. Sympathetic hyperactivity often results in decreased circulation (ischemia) to the muscles, nerves, and other structures, which contributes to pain.

Another advantage of a nerve block injection is that allows a damaged nerve time to heal. There is also a diagnostic advantage—by performing a nerve block and then monitoring how the patient responds to the injection, I can glean information to help me determine the cause or source of the pain.

Various types of pain disorders commonly treated with nerve blocks include herpetic neuralgia, intercostal neuralgia, trigeminal neuralgia, sciatica, piriformis syndrome, metatarsalgia, carpel tunnel syndrome, pain of the lumbar or cervical radiculopathy, lower back pain, reflex sympathetic dystrophy or complex regional syndrome, diabetic pain, cervical and lumbar entrapment neuropathy, diabetic neuropathy, peripheral neuropathy, and many others.

I am trained to provide many different types of nerve blocks, including individual nerve blocks, bier blocks, stellate ganglion blocks, epidural blocks, intercostal nerve blocks, sacral nerve root blocks, and others. Sympathetic and sacral nerve root blocks have proven to be of great value in my practice, especially in treating lower back and lower extremity pain, pelvic pain, myofascial pain, diabetic pain and peripheral neuropathy, pain resulting from peripheral vascular disease, and many others. I have commonly utilized sympathetic and sacral nerve root blocks at multiple levels for improvement of peripheral circulation and pain relief, with outstanding results. The anesthetic agent commonly used to block these nerves is lidocaine 1%. Utmost discretion should be exercised in using steroids with nerve blocks because of their harmful side effects.

The physician utilizing the nerve block must be fully trained as a qualified pain specialist (fellowship trained and certified), with special training in anesthesia or fellowship training in regional anesthesia. There are a few specialties, such as physical medicine and rehabilitation, anesthesiology, neurology, and psychiatry, which offer physician's board certification in pain management based on theoretical testing, but without any hands-on training to acquire the necessary skills to provide optimal, effective, and specialized care. This lack of appropriate training leads to more confusion for the pain patient, who desperately seeks much needed pain relief. As an experienced and fellowship trained pain specialist, I truly feel that a fellowship in pain management must be mandatory for a pain specialist to provide appropriate and specialized care, and to have the right credentials to market him or herself as a true specialist.

The pain physician must perform a thorough history and physical examination and make a concrete diagnosis before administering any type of nerve block or other treatments. The doctor must have full knowledge of the anatomy of the area of the nerve block, the pharmacology of the local anesthetic, and the side effects and complications that can result from these procedures. Physicians must be fully capable of effectively handling all the complications that could possibly result from the administration of different types of nerve blocks or other procedures. Emergency equipment must be at hand to take care of any complications.

Trigger point injections

As discussed earlier, myofascial trigger points are areas of hyperirritability in the muscle or its fascia, responsible for causing pain locally or in the zone of reference. Trigger points can also develop in the periosteum, tendons, ligaments, and scar tissue as well. Myofascial trigger point injections (TPI) are a procedure used to deactivate the trigger points, those painful knots of muscle that form when muscles do not relax. Trigger point injections are performed with the patient lying down. The injection contains a local anesthetic solution, like novocaine or lidocaine. With the injection, the trigger point is made inactive and the pain is alleviated. The course of treatment will usually result in sustained relief, but it can vary from individual to individual. Injections usually take just a few minutes and several sites may be injected at once. Repeated treatments with trigger point injections are usually needed and can accomplish long-term, positive results.

An alternate therapy to trigger point injections is called spray and stretch. It can also be helpful, but results can be less than optimal. Some doctors prefer to do dry needling of the muscle, which often has limited results.

Physical rehabilitation, including strengthening and stretching exercises

Physical therapy and rehabilitation are important parts of my Dynamic Model. Patients suffering from chronic pain often develop associated physical disabilities, leading to a decrease in or loss of functionality in the ability to walk, bend, use stairs, or perform routine errands, such as grocery shopping or simple chores.

Relieving a patient's pain without restoring his or her lost functionality is like going to a temple without praying or doing a job only halfway.

The goals of therapeutic exercises include improving and maintaining strength, endurance, circulation, elasticity, range of motion, joint mobility, balance and coordination, posture, and proprioception (bodily awareness), among others. These goals are achieved through strengthening and stretching exercises and actively resisted exercises (the movement or exercise of the body against a resisting force), which increase power, strength, and neuromuscular and cardiovascular conditioning. In addition, I recommend walking alternated with jogging. It helps improve an individual's physical stamina and often results in a reduction of weight.

Daily exercises not only keep patients engaged in their own active care, but also help with the release of endorphins, a natural opioid, which relieves symptoms of depression and increases stamina.

Daily stretching helps deactivate trigger point activity, which is often the cause of pain, muscle weakness, and limitation in range of motion, and often results from deconditioning of muscles from lack of daily exercise, a sedentary lifestyle, or being overweight.

Adjunctive treatments like hot packs, electrical stimulation

The application of heat by means of a heat pack can often control pain and speed the healing process. The application of heat interferes with pain signals being sent through your spine to the brain, especially neuropathic pain. Moist heat is commonly used in my practice.

Along with increasing muscle strength, heat relaxes muscles, which promotes blood supply to the area and assists in healing. The additional benefits of heat include muscle relaxation, increased vaso-dilation, increased circulation, increased oxygenation of muscles and other tissues, elimination of tissue waste products via the process of sweating, and analgesia.

Some physicians use deep heat, such as ultrasound, shortwave diathermy, and microwave diathermy. Unfortunately, the long-term benefit and therapeutic effects can be very limited and pain relief less than optimal. Therefore, I do not often use such treatments.

Electrical stimulation of the skin is commonly used in my center as an adjunctive modality, primarily to excite the peripheral nerves to produce analgesia and improve microcirculation to the muscles. Though patients like its soothing and relaxing effects, it has limited therapeutic value because of the complexity and multiple causes of pain.

Therapeutic massage also falls under the category of adjunctive treatments. It has a transitory yet soothing feeling, but long-term ben-efits are limited. The sense of touch, aided by deep tissue manipula-tion, helps improve the circulation to the muscles, produces general relaxation and sedation, as well as a certain amount of analgesia for a short duration because of the release of endorphins, but it often fails to break the cycle of pain which is essential for long term pain relief.

Chronic pain patients often undergo deep implantation of elec-trodes under the skin or in the epidural space with very limited results. This intervention often leads to more iatrogenic complications, dis-ability, and pain.

I firmly believe that such interventions should be avoided. They sound fancy, but often are counter productive in achieving long lasting pain relief. Any unnecessary surgical or non-surgical interventions can often exacerbate chronic pain and disability.

Psychotherapy (individual, family, group)

The psychological and psychiatric treatment of chronic pain patients is an essential part of my Dynamic Model. As discussed, the Bio-Psychosocial Model of illness understands the clear link between body and mind in evaluating and treating pain. In addition, the basic definition of pain states that it is an unpleasant emotional and sensory experience associated with actual or potential tissue damage. Viewed in this way, pain is profoundly linked to psychological issues and implications.

In fact, the emotional or psychological component is often more complex than this basic definition. Very often pain patients can be very depressed because of changes in their neurophysiology. They experience frustration and depression from repeated failures to achieve significant pain relief after various invasive and non-invasive interventions. Physicians and health care providers, working from the obsolete biomedical or dualistic model, treat pain as a figment of the patient's imagination if x-rays or scans come back negative. Chronic pain patients get labeled as "malingerers" or "crazy," and are often told to see a psychiatrist. No wonder so many pain patients are depressed. This kind of treatment can even lead, on occasion, to suicide.

When a patient comes to my center, my wife, Dr. Sukhveen Kaur Ajrawat, conducts a thorough evaluation and reviews every aspect of the patient's life that is pertinent to his or her physical illness. This includes family life, work setting, social setting, children, finances, self-esteem, relationships, compensation issues, the patient's motivation, and many other issues.

After a thorough evaluation and concrete diagnosis, the patient is gently guided to participate in individual, group, and family therapy. The patient's workplace is often contacted to ensure that the employer understands that the patient needs professional care and must not be judged harshly. Proper communication on various fronts, along with proper physical and psychological treatment, is therapeutically effective in returning the patient to a functional lifestyle. Usually, in a relatively short time, a patient who felt shunned and disenfranchised develops a sense of belonging, self-assurance, and purpose in living his or her life to its fullest potential.

Various therapeutic approaches are used, including operant conditioning and behavioral modification. In addition, patient education and improving the patient's self esteem are two very important components of our psychotherapeutic approaches. Use of pharmacotherapeutic approaches, such antidepressants, analgesics (narcotic and non-narcotic), natural thyroid preparation, and others are commonly used, following controlled and stringent criteria. Top priority is given to reducing side effects from pharmacological agents, and to the patient's compliance with dose schedules.

In my training as a fellow in pain management, I learned many techniques, such as Biofeedback, medical hypnosis, and relaxation exercises, which I used in the early part of my practice in pain management. But in recent years they have been replaced by my air-pulse autonomic meditation therapy, which has proven much more effective and less time consuming in treating pain patients.

This specialized and interdisciplinary approach to treating the whole person—body and mind—has been very effective in providing lasting pain relief.

Pharmacotherapy (use of narcotic, non-narcotic analgesics, antidepressants and others)

Medication can serve an important role in treatment. However, in too many cases, patients are overmedicated for conditions that can be treated in other ways. For example, a patient named John came to see me, suffering from panic attacks, headaches, and depression. He had been taking over-the-counter medications for these problems for many years before he saw me. He was prescribed demerol, imitrex, morphine, and other medications by his doctors, but still John's problems persisted. I reduced the medications John was taking and put him through a regimen of injection therapy, meditation therapy, and exercise. John's health began to improve dramatically, and he was

able to lead a pain-free life without excessive dependence on medication. John is now free from headaches, panic attacks, and depression,
feels very grateful and appreciative, and has become an enthusiastic
advocate of these holistic treatments.

Ajrawat Air-Pulse Autonomic Therapy

With all patients, whether suffering from chronic physical pain or
day to day stress, I use Ajrawat Air-Pulse Autonomic Therapy. I have
discussed in previous chapters how it works.

The positive effects of my meditation therapy open a new frontier
to help people confronted with pain, stress, or any other medical problem detrimental to one's sense of total well being. It restores the body
to normalcy, to the effective and dynamic state it originally possessed
at birth. Once the body returns to that optimal state, it is ready to
merge and unify with its microcosmic/ macrocosmic source. Through
this therapy, energy is physically optimized within the human mind
and body, which takes functioning and awareness to a new level of
spirituality and self-realization. Yet another physiological phenomena
takes place—the merging of unitary consciousness with a much more
expansive source of energy, the greater consciousness. You return to
your original self and soul—a true homecoming. This experience will
be discussed in detail in Chapter Six.

Combined with other components of my pain treatment plan, such
as varied and regular exercise, walking alternated with jogging, balanced nutrition, strengthening and stretching exercises, a disciplined
lifestyle, and the practice of correct principles, one can achieve not
only a physically healthy mind and body, but also a self-actualized and
empowered self as well.

In the next chapter, we will look at how my revolutionary therapeutic techniques have successfully addressed a wide range of physical and emotional ailments.

PRESS RELEASE

--For Immediate Release

Dr. P.S. Ajrawat, a pioneer and a qualified pain specialist introduces the first scientific meditation therapy in the world in his book,

"The Autonomic Healing of Self-Dr. Ajrawat's Air-Pulse Autonomic Meditation Therapy"

New Book to Announce a Revolutionary New Therapy for Treating Pain and Stress

At the same time, Autonomic Meditation Therapy can be used in combination with more traditional treatment methods, such psychotherapy and medication, to address more serious and complicated emotional and psychological problems, such as posttraumatic stress disorder (PTSD), attention deficit disorder (ADD), obsessive-compulsive disorder (OCD), schizophrenia, and others.

As new brain research shows, most psychological disorders are the result of structural changes in the brain. Any individual can develop problems in brain circuitry, which can perpetuate negative thoughts and behaviors and exacerbate physical illnesses. Autonomic Meditation Therapy breaks that cycle by literally washing away flawed circuitry, while establishing new circuits and links in the memory cycle. In short, Autonomic Meditation Therapy cleanses mind and body from old and negative conditioning.

Chapter 5

Treating Specific Emotional, Psychiatric, and Physical Disorders

I have spent the previous chapters telling you about the theories behind my work, but in the end this is primarily a book about solutions. It is designed to help you, the reader, get help for your problems, whether you suffer from common emotional problems like stress and anxiety, or whether you suffer from more serious problems associated with chronic physical pain. I firmly believe that every kind of emotional and physical pain can be properly treated, and in this chapter I will describe, in detail, how my methods have successfully remedied over two-dozen conditions.

For each condition I provide the following information, giving you a thorough overview of each disorder's causes and symptoms and how I treat it.

1) Definition. I clearly define the disorder. There is much misconception and misunderstanding about many disorders, and I clarify the confusion.

2) Symptoms, causes, and risk factors. I describe the disorder's symptoms, which are often misunderstood or misinterpreted by traditional medical approaches. Then I describe what causes the disorder and the risk factors involved.

3) Evaluation, diagnosis, and treatment. I describe how I evaluate and correctly diagnose the disorder, and the specific treatments I use to alleviate and treat it.

I have organized these disorders into three categories:

1) Common emotional disorders, such as stress, anxiety, panic disorder, and depression.

2) More serious emotional disorders, such as PTSD, phobias, obsessive-compulsive disorder, and others.

3) Chronic physical disorders, such as myofascial pain, fibromyalgia, neck and shoulder pain, frozen shoulders, rotator cuff tears, headaches, back pain, hip pain, leg pain, knee pain, carpel tunnel syndrome, flat or pigeon feet pain, metatarsalgia, reflex sympathetic dystrophy, diabetic neuropathy, peripheral neuropathy, cancer pain, and many others.

In short, this chapter is organized so that we start with the most common emotional problems, which can be treated largely through Ajrawat Air-Pulse Autonomic Therapy, such as stress, anxiety, panic disorder, depression, and ADD, and proceed to the more serious and chronic emotional and physical disorders, such as narcissism and schizophrenia, herniated disks and arthritis, which can be treated through my multi-modality treatment model.

In doing so, I hope to debunk myths about illness that originate in the outdated medical model. For example, under the old treatment model, both migraine headaches and arthritis was commonly perceived to be among the most common physical disorders. But, in fact, what has been diagnosed in the past as migraine headaches or arthritis is really the result of myofascial pain and must be understood and treated in that way to bring lasting relief.

The old frames of reference for the evaluation and treatment of pain are indeed obsolete and counterproductive. They must be challenged and eventually discarded in favor of newer frames of reference. My approach to pain management is more comprehensive, multidimensional, natural, and autonomous than traditional approaches.

Now, as you read about my treatment approaches to specific illnesses, you will understand even more why my methods are truly revolutionary in nature and offer new hope to millions of pain sufferers.

Treating Common Emotional Disorders

Anxiety

Definition: What is Generalized Anxiety Disorder?

Generalized anxiety disorder (or GAD) is characterized by excessive, exaggerated anxiety and worry about everyday life events with no obvious reasons for worry. People with this disorder tend to always expect disaster and can't stop worrying about health, money, family, work, or school. The worry often is unrealistic or out of proportion for the situation. Daily life becomes a constant state of fear and dread. Eventually, the anxiety so dominates the person's thinking that it interferes with daily functioning, including work, school, social activities, and relationships.

About 6.5 million adult Americans suffer from GAD. It most often begins in childhood or adolescence, but can begin in adulthood, and is more common in women than in men.

Symptoms, Causes, and Risk Factors

Symptoms of GAD can include: excessive, ongoing worry and tension, an unrealistic view of problems, restlessness or a feeling of being "edgy," irritability, muscle tension, headaches, difficulty concentrating or sleeping, and being easily startled

In addition, people with GAD often have other anxiety disorders (such as panic disorder, obsessive-compulsive disorder, and phobias), suffer from depression, and/or abuse drugs or alcohol.

The exact cause of GAD is not fully known, but a number of factors—including genetics, brain chemistry, and environmental stresses—appear to contribute to its development. Some research suggests that family history plays a part in increasing the likelihood that a person will develop GAD. In addition, GAD has been associated with abnormal levels of certain neurotransmitters in the brain. This can alter the way the brain reacts in certain situations, leading to anxiety. Finally, trauma and stressful events may lead to GAD.

Evaluation, Diagnosis, and Treatment

Although there are no laboratory tests to specifically diagnose anxiety disorders, I use various tests to look for physical illness as the cause of the symptoms. I also look for emotional or psychological causes that can be treated through autonomic therapy, psychotherapy, and medication.

As we saw from the case of Sandra in Chapter One, physical ailments cannot be healed unless the entire person is healed, and that includes the person's emotional and psychological state.

Panic attacks

Definition: What are panic attacks?

At least 20% of adult Americans, or about 60 million people, will suffer from panic attacks at some point in their lives. About 1.7% of adult Americans, or about 3 million people, will have a full-blown panic disorder at some point. A panic attack is strikingly different from general anxiety: attacks are sudden and often unexpected, appear to be unprovoked, and are often disabling.

Once someone has had a panic attack while driving, shopping in a crowded store, or riding in an elevator, he or she may develop irrational fears, called phobias, about these situations and begin to avoid them. Eventually, the pattern of avoidance and level of anxiety about another attack may reach the point at which the mere idea of doing things that preceded the first panic attack triggers future panic attacks, resulting in the individual with panic disorder being unable to drive or even step out of the house. At this stage, the person is said to have panic disorder with agoraphobia.

Symptoms, Causes, and Risk Factors

Symptoms of a panic attack may include racing or pounding heartbeat, chest pains, difficulty breathing, trembling and shaking, dreamlike sensations or perceptual distortions, a sense that something unimaginably horrible is about to occur and one is powerless to prevent it, and fear of dying. Without treatment, panic attacks tend to continue for months or years.

Typically, most people who have one attack will have others, and when someone has repeated attacks with no other apparent physical or emotional cause, or feels severe anxiety about having another attack, he or she is said to have panic disorder. A number of other emotional problems can have panic attacks as a symptom. Some of these illnesses include posttraumatic stress disorder (PTSD), schizophrenia, and intoxication or withdrawal from certain drugs of abuse.

Although there is no one specific cause for panic attacks, they are understood to be the result of a combination of biological vulnerabilities, ways of thinking, and social stressors. According to one theory of panic disorder, the body's normal "alarm system," the set of mental and physical mechanisms that allows a person to respond to a threat, tends to be triggered unnecessarily, when there is no danger. Scientists don't know exactly why this happens or why some people are more susceptible to the problem than others.

Psychologically, people who develop panic attacks or an anxiety disorder are more likely to have a history of what is known as anxiety sensitivity. Anxiety sensitivity is the tendency for a person to fear that anxiety-related bodily sensations (like brief chest pain) have dire personal consequences (for example, believing that it automatically means their heart will stop).

From a social standpoint, a risk factor for developing panic disorder as an adolescent or adult is a history of being physically or sexually abused as a child. Often, the first attacks are triggered by physical illnesses, another major life stress, or perhaps medications that increase activity in the part of the brain involved in fear reactions.

Evaluation, Diagnosis, and Treatment

Because of the disturbing physical signs and symptoms that accompany panic attacks, they may be mistaken for heart attacks or some other life-threatening medical illness. In fact, up to 25% of people who visit emergency rooms because of chest pain are actually experiencing panic. As a result, people with this symptom often undergo extensive medical tests to rule out these other conditions. Sadly, sometimes more than 90% of these individuals are not appropriately diagnosed as suffering from panic.

Medical personnel generally attempt to reassure the panic attack sufferer that he or she is not in great danger. But these efforts at reassurance can sometimes add to the patient's difficulties. If doctors use expressions such as "nothing serious," "all in your head," or "nothing to worry about," this may give the incorrect impression that there is no real problem, that they should be able to overcome their symptoms on their own, and that treatment is not possible or necessary.

Panic attacks are real and potentially quite emotionally disabling, but they can be controlled with specific treatments.

John is one such example. He was suffering from headaches, depression, and panic disorders. He started having these problems in 1985 and started taking over-the-counter medications that didn't help his problems. Numerous doctors prescribed a variety of drugs, including demerol, morphine, and others he can't recall. After having headaches for two to three weeks, a doctor suggested he seek me out for alternative treatments.

"I made the choice to go and see if he could help me," John says. "Anything had to be better then taking Imitrex for the long term answer. Dr. Ajrawat talked to me at length about my past meds and treatments and said he could show me a better way to relieve my problems. After his injection therapy, meditation therapy, and exercise my headaches are better and I haven't suffered a panic attack in a long time. I surely have a much better life at this time."

Depression

Definition: What is a depressive disorder?

In the 19th century, depression was seen as an inherited weakness of temperament. In the first half of the 20th century, Freud linked the development of depression to guilt and conflict. John Cheever, the author and a modern sufferer of depressive disorder, wrote of conflict and experiences with his parents as influencing his development of depression.

In the 1950s and 60s, depression was divided into two types, endogenous and neurotic. Endogenous means that the depression comes from within the body, perhaps of genetic origin, or comes out of nowhere. Neurotic or reactive depression has a clear environmental precipitating factor, such as the death of a spouse, or other significant loss, such as the loss of a job.

Depressive disorders are a huge public-health problem, affecting millions of people. About 10% of adults, up to 8% of teens, and 2% of preteen children experience some kind of depressive disorder.

The statistics on the costs due to depression in the United States include huge amounts of direct costs, which are for treatment, and indirect costs, such as lost productivity and absenteeism from work or school.

Depression can increase the risks for developing coronary artery disease, HIV, asthma, and many other medical illnesses.

One of the most common myths about depression is that it's a weakness rather than an illness, and that if the sufferer just tries hard enough, it will go away.

Symptoms, Causes, and Risk Factors

Not everyone who is depressed experiences every symptom. Some people experience a few symptoms and some many symptoms. The severity of symptoms also varies with individuals. Common symptoms of depression include: persistently feeling sad, anxious, angry, or irritable, feelings of hopelessness, pessimism, loss of interest or pleasure in hobbies and activities that were once enjoyed, including sex, restlessness, irritability, inability to concentrate, insomnia, social isolation, decreased appetite, fatigue, and thoughts of suicide or suicide attempts.

Some types of depression run in families, indicating that it can be inherited.

An external event often seems to initiate an episode of depression. Thus, a serious loss, chronic illness, chronic pain (such as myofascial pain), a difficult relationship, a financial problem, or any unwelcome change in life patterns can trigger a depressive episode. Very often, a combination of genetic, psychological, and environmental factors is involved in the onset of the disorder. Seasonal affective disorder, psychotic depression, post partum depression, and bipolar disorder are additional causes.

Stressors that contribute to the development of depression sometimes affect some groups more than others. For example, minority groups who more often feel impacted by discrimination are disproportionately represented. Socioeconomically disadvantaged groups have higher rates of depression compared to their advantaged counterparts. Immigrants to the United States may be more vulnerable to developing depression, particularly when isolated by language.

Women are twice as likely to become depressed as men. However, scientists do not know the reason for this difference. Psychological factors also contribute to a person's vulnerability to depression. Thus, persistent deprivation in infancy, physical or sexual abuse, clusters of certain personality traits, and inadequate ways of coping (maladaptive coping mechanisms) all can increase the frequency and severity of depressive disorders, with or without inherited vulnerability.

Evaluation, Diagnosis, and Treatment

Justin had chronic foot problems for years, even after seeing an excellent podiatrist. He altered his walking pattern due to the pain he was feeling in his feet, which in turn exacerbated his gout. On top of that, Justin suffered depression for years.

On the first day I saw Justin, I corrected the orthopedic inserts he used to compensate for slight leg shortness and to achieve better arch support. The effect was immediately noticeable. Justin started to walk more naturally and easily, and even the uneven wear patterns in his shoes started to disappear. I then concentrated on working with the muscle groups that were still giving him myofascial pain, all the way from his legs up to his shoulders, using sympathetic nerve blocks, trigger point injections, and my air-pulse autonomic therapy. Along with my program of combined heat and electronic stimulation therapy, in conjunction with regular therapeutic exercise, I helped to alleviate the muscle pain that Justin experienced from the strain of being active again.

Justin then started jogging, alternated with walking, to reduce his weight and the subsequent stress on his joints, as well as strengthen his muscles. Almost all of Justin's pain disappeared and he lost over 50 pounds.

"After spending days or even weeks at a time stuck on the couch with swollen feet," he says, "I now have the freedom to get on with my life, work, and attend events I had missed for a long time. I even was able to pursue sports that I never thought I would play again.

"While Dr. Ajrawat was treating my pain, he also taught me how to use air pulse meditation therapy. It is very effective and quite simple—simple enough that I can do it almost anywhere to ward off stress and depression, so I can keep motivated and go about my day. Using controlled breathing along with feeling my pulse lets me reduce my blood pressure and stress whenever I need too. I've also found out that smiling is one of the best medicines and really works wonders. I've since learned to use mental images and my own reflection to achieve the same effect. The total effect of this treatment has completely changed my life and allowed me to follow my dreams to their fullest potential."

Since my autonomic therapy stimulates parasympathetic activity, resulting in vasodilation, it can help heal damaged areas of the brain naturally or in combination with antidepressant and antipsychotic medications.

Treating More Serious Emotional Disorders

Obsessive Compulsive Disorder (<u>OCD</u>)

Definition: What is obsessive compulsive disorder?

Obsessive compulsive disorder (OCD) is an anxiety disorder that is characterized repeated obsessions and/or compulsions that interfere with the person's ability to function socially, occupationally, or educationally, either as a result of the amount of time that is consumed by the symptoms or the marked fear or other distress suffered by the person.

Statistics on the number of people in the United States who have OCD range from 1%-2%, or more than 2 to 3 million adults.

Symptoms, Causes, and Risk Factors

An obsession is defined as a thought, impulse, or image that either recurs or persists and causes severe anxiety. These thoughts are irresistible to the OCD sufferer despite the person's realizing that these thoughts are irrational. Examples of obsessions include worries about germs/cleanliness or about safety or order. A compulsion is a ritual/behavior that the individual with OCD engages in repeatedly, either because of their obsessions or according to a rigid set of rules. The obsessions may result in compulsions like excessive hand washing, skin picking, lock checking, or repeatedly arranging items.

While there is no known specific cause for OCD, family history and chemical imbalances in the brain are thought to contribute to the development of the illness. A specific chromosome/gene variation has been found to possibly double the likelihood of a person developing OCD. It is thought that an imbalance of the chemical serotonin in the brain may also contribute to its development.

Without treatment, the symptoms of OCD can progress to the point that the sufferer's life becomes consumed, inhibiting their ability to keep a job and maintain important relationships. Many people with OCD have thoughts of killing themselves, and about 1% complete suicide.

Evaluation, Diagnosis, and Treatment

In addition to conducting a mental-status examination, I will explore the possibility that the individual is suffering from another emotional illness instead of or in addition to OCD. I will also conduct a physical examination to determine whether there is any medical problem that could be contributing to the signs of OCD.

Attention deficit hyperactivity disorder (ADHD)

Definition: What is attention deficit hyperactivity disorder (ADHD)?

ADHD refers to a chronic biobehavioral disorder that initially manifests in childhood and is characterized by hyperactivity, impulsivity, and/or inattention (although not all of those affected by ADHD manifest all three behavioral categories). These symptoms can lead to difficulty in academic, emotional, and social functioning. Head trauma often can cause or aggravate ADHD.

Studies in the United States indicate approximately 8%-10% of children have ADHD. It is therefore one of the most common disorders of childhood. While previously believed to be "outgrown" by adulthood, current opinion indicates that many symptoms will continue throughout life.

Symptoms, Causes, and Risk Factors

The causes of ADHD are not completely clear. One theory postulates that differences in brain chemistry can affect judgment, impulse control, alertness, planning, and mental flexibility. In addition, a genetic predisposition has been demonstrated in (identical) twin and sibling studies.

The diagnostic criteria for ADHD are outlined in the *Diagnostic and Statistical Manual of Mental Health, 4th ed.* (*DSM-IV*). The symptoms of inattention, hyperactivity, and impulsivity must have appeared before age seven, persisted for at least six months, and result in clear evidence of significant impairment in social, academic, or occupational functioning. Among the symptomatic behaviors are the following:

- The child often fails to give close attention to details or makes careless mistakes in schoolwork, work, or other activities.
- The child often has difficulty sustaining attention in tasks or play activities.
- The child often does not seem to listen when spoken to directly.

- The child often does not follow through on instructions and fails to finish schoolwork, chores, or duties in the workplace (not due to oppositional behavior or failure to understand instructions).

Evaluation, Diagnosis, and Treatment

Evaluation and diagnosis of ADHD can be difficult, because it often is present with co-existing conditions, such as oppositional defiant disorder (ODD), mood disorders, like depression, anxiety disorders, and learning disorders.

As with OCD, I will explore the possibility that the individual is suffering from another emotional illness instead of or in addition to ADHD. I will also conduct a physical examination to determine whether there is any medical problem that could be contributing to the signs of ADHD.

<u>Posttraumatic stress disorder (PTSD)</u>

Definition: What is posttraumatic stress disorder (PTSD)?

Posttraumatic stress disorder (PTSD is an emotional illness that usually develops as a result of a terribly frightening, life-threatening, or otherwise highly unsafe experience. PTSD sufferers re-experience the traumatic event or events in some way, tend to avoid places, people, or other things that remind them of the event, and are exquisitely sensitive to normal life experiences. Long before it was an official diagnosis, veterans of combat suffered from what is now known as PTSD.

Approximately 7%-8% of people in the United States will likely develop PTSD in their lifetime, with prevalence in combat veterans and rape victims. Somewhat higher rates of this disorder have been found to occur in African Americans, Hispanics, and Native Americans. Women are twice as likely as men to develop PTSD.

As evidenced by the occurrence of stress in many individuals in the United States in the days following the 2001 terrorist attacks, not being physically present at a traumatic event does not guarantee that one cannot suffer from traumatic stress that can lead to the development of PTSD. Up to 100% of children who have seen a parent killed or endured sexual assault or abuse tend to develop PTSD, and more than one-third of youths who are exposed to community violence (for example, a shooting, stabbing, or other assault) will suffer from the disorder.

Symptoms, Causes, and Risk Factors

Three groups of symptoms are required to assign the diagnosis of PTSD:

- recurrent episodes of re-experiencing of the trauma (for example, troublesome memories, flashbacks, recurring nightmares, and/or dissociative reliving of the trauma).
- avoidance to the point of having a phobia of places, people, and experiences that remind the sufferer of the trauma and a general numbing of emotional responsiveness.
- chronic physical signs of hyperarousal, including sleep problems, trouble concentrating, irritability, anger, poor concentration, blackouts or difficulty remembering things, increased tendency and reaction to being startled, and hypervigilance to threat.

Issues that tend to put people at higher risk for developing PTSD include increased duration of a traumatic event, higher number of traumatic events endured, higher severity of the trauma experienced, having an emotional condition prior to the event, or having little social support in the form of family or friends. In addition to those risk factors, children and adolescents, females, and people with learning disabilities or violence in the home seem to have a greater risk of developing PTSD after a traumatic event.

Evaluation, Diagnosis, and Treatment

Diagnosis of PTSD can be difficult for practitioners to make since sufferers often complain of symptoms associated with other conditions, such as depression or drug addiction.

My wife and I treat PTSD through a combination of approaches. For example, individual or group cognitive behavioral psychotherapy at my pain management center can help people with PTSD recognize and adjust trauma-related thoughts. They learn to understand the relationship between thoughts and feelings, develop alternative interpretations, and practice new ways of looking at things.

We also directly address the sleep problems that can be part of PTSD. Specifically, rehearsing adaptive ways of coping with nightmares (imagery rehearsal therapy), meditation therapy, positive self-talk, and screening for other sleep problems have been found to be particularly helpful in decreasing the sleep problems associated with PTSD.

Other treatment methods include reducing stress through meditation therapy and incorporating positive lifestyle practices (for example, exercise, healthy eating, and volunteering).

As you saw in the first chapter, Sandra was a vivid example of someone who was suffering from PTSD after the murder of her son. Sandra developed physical health problems that were exacerbated by her PTSD, and in turn her PTSD became worse because of her physical problems. Until both her emotional and physical problems were treated in a holistic and interrelated way, Sandra could not recover her health in either domain.

In addition to the psychological disorders described above, we also treat phobias, narcissism, autism, and schizophrenia. Here is a look at the definition, causes, symptoms, and risk factors for each.

Phobias

Definition: What is a phobia?

A phobia is defined as the unrelenting fear of a situation, activity, or thing that causes one to want to avoid it. The three kinds of phobias are social phobia (fear of public speaking, meeting new people, or other social situations), agoraphobia (fear of being outside), and specific phobias (fear of particular items or situations).

Phobias are largely underreported, probably because many phobia sufferers find ways to avoid the situations to which they are phobic. Therefore, statistics that estimate how many people suffer from phobias vary widely, but at minimum, phobias afflict more than 6 million people in the United States. These illnesses have been thought to affect up to 28 out of every 100 people. Women tend to be twice as likely to suffer from a phobia compared to men.

Symptoms, Causes, and Risk Factors

Symptoms of phobias often involve having feelings of panic, dread, or terror, despite recognition that those feelings are excessive in relationship to any real danger, as well as physical symptoms like shaking, rapid heart beat, trouble breathing, and an overwhelming desire to escape the situation that is causing the phobic reaction.

While there is no one specific known cause for phobias, it is thought that phobias run in families, are influenced by culture, and can be triggered by life events. Immediate family members of people with phobias are about three times more likely to also suffer from a phobia than those who do not have such a family history. Phobia sufferers have been found to be more likely to manage stress by avoiding the stressful situation and to have difficulty minimizing the intensity of the fearful situation.

<u>Narcissism</u>

Definition: What is narcissism?

Narcissism is a term used to describe a focus on the self and self-admiration that is taken to an extreme. The word "narcissism" comes from a Greek myth in which a handsome young man named Narcissus sees his reflection in a pool of water and falls in love with it.

Narcissistic personality disorder is one of a group of conditions called dramatic personality disorders. People with these disorders have intense, unstable emotions and a distorted self-image. Narcissistic personality disorder is further characterized by an abnormal love of self, an exaggerated sense of superiority and importance, and a preoccupation with success and power. However, these attitudes and behaviors do not reflect true self-confidence. Instead, the attitudes conceal a deep sense of insecurity and a fragile self-esteem.

Symptoms, Causes, and Risk Factors

In many cases, people with narcissistic personality disorder are self-centered and boastful, seek constant attention and admiration, consider themselves better than others, exaggerate their talents and achievements, and believe that they are entitled to special treatment.

The exact cause of narcissistic personality disorder is not known. However, many mental health professionals believe it results from extremes in child rearing. For example, the disorder might develop as the result of excessive pampering, or when a child's parents have a need for their children to be talented or special in order to maintain their own self-esteem. On the other end of the spectrum, narcissistic personality disorder might develop as the result of neglect or abuse and trauma inflicted by parents or other authority figures during childhood.

The disorder usually is evident by early adulthood. People with narcissistic personality disorder might abuse drugs and/or alcohol as a way of coping with their symptoms. The disorder also might interfere with the development of healthy relationships with others.

Schizophrenia

Definition: What is schizophrenia?

Schizophrenia is a chronic, severe, and disabling brain disorder that affects about 1% of Americans.

People with the disorder may hear voices other people don't hear. They may believe other people are reading their minds, controlling their thoughts, or plotting to harm them. This can terrify people with the illness and make them withdrawn or extremely agitated.

People with schizophrenia may not make sense when they talk. They may sit for hours without moving or talking. Sometimes people with schizophrenia seem perfectly fine until they talk about what they are really thinking.

Families and society are deeply affected by schizophrenia. Treatment helps relieve many symptoms of schizophrenia, but most people who have the disorder cope with symptoms throughout their lives.

Symptoms, Causes, and Risk Factors

The symptoms of schizophrenia include hallucinations, delusions, difficulty organizing thoughts, and movement disorders. Additional symptoms include disruptions to normal emotions and behaviors. These symptoms are harder to recognize as part of the disorder and can be mistaken for depression or other conditions. These symptoms include flat affect, lack of pleasure in everyday life, lack of ability to begin and sustain planned activities, and speaking little, even when forced to interact.

People with schizophrenia need help with everyday tasks. They often neglect basic personal hygiene. This may make them seem lazy or unwilling to help themselves, but the problems are symptoms caused by the schizophrenia.

Schizophrenia affects men and women equally. It occurs at similar rates in all ethnic groups around the world. Symptoms such as hallucinations and delusions usually start between ages 16 and 30. Men tend to experience symptoms a little earlier than women. Most of the time, people do not get schizophrenia after age 45. Schizophrenia rarely occurs in children, but awareness of childhood-onset schizophrenia is increasing.

Experts think schizophrenia is caused by these factors.

- Genes and environment. Scientists have long known that schizophrenia runs in families. Scientists believe several genes are associated with an increased risk of schizophrenia, but that no gene causes the disease by itself.
- Different brain chemistry and structure. Scientists think that an imbalance in the complex, interrelated chemical reactions of the brain involving the neurotransmitters dopamine and glutamate, and possibly others, plays a role in schizophrenia.

Treating Chronic Physical Disorders

Here I describe how I treat a range of physical disorders.

Myofascial Pain Syndrome

Definition: What is myofascial pain?

Myofascial pain is commonly overlooked or neglected, yet it is the major cause of pain and dysfunction in the body. Nearly everyone experiences muscle pain from time to time that generally resolves in a few days. But people with myofascial pain disorder have muscular and fascial pain that persists or worsens, becoming chronic in nature and disrupting their lives.

Muscles make up the major bulk of human body weight. As a system, they are instrumental in collectively mobilizing, balancing, and coordinating bodily movements and functions, both voluntary and involuntary. Fascia is a layer of fibrous tissue that interpenetrates the entire body, surrounding muscles, bones, organs, nerves, blood vessels, and other structures.

Contrary to popular belief, the muscles and fascia are the bodily tissues that suffer the most wear and tear as the body ages, and not the bones, discs, or nerves. Yet most healthcare professionals generally tend to focus on the latter and ignore the former.

As a result, most physicians and healthcare providers have received little or no training in treating myofascial pain. This is unfortunate, because in most cases it can be eliminated and full function of the body restored.

Symptoms, Causes, and Risk Factors

The most common and characteristic symptom of myofascial pain is a dull, aching, and often deep pain, its intensity varying from mere discomfort to severe, debilitating pain. This pain can be experienced in specific patterns characteristic to each muscle; it can be localized to one part of the body or it can be generalized. The most common symptoms are presented in the neck, shoulders, upper extremities, facial area, lower back, and lower extremities. About two-thirds of patients state that they "hurt all over."

Poor sleep is common with myofascial pain. Some 80% of patients complain of "morning fatigue" and generalized weakness.

Sensitive areas of tight fibers can form in your muscles after injuries or overuse. These sensitive areas are called trigger points, which cause pain when they become inflamed. A trigger point (TP) can be active or latent.

An active TP produces pain with any movement of the muscle that stretches it, but also during rest as well. An active TP is always tender and usually weakens the muscle, producing a "twitch response" when palpated directly.

A latent TP does not cause pain during normal daily activities, but only when palpated. In addition, a latent TP can cause limitations in range of motion, such as difficulty when bending.

Factors that may increase your risk of muscle trigger points include:

- **Mechanical stress or skeletal disproportion**, such as a short leg, short hemi-pelvis, long second metatarsal bone, or rounded shoulders.
- **Psychological stressors.** Depression, anxiety, "Mary Martyr" or "Good Sport" syndrome, poor sleep.
- **Postural stressors.** Poorly designed furniture, like chairs without proper back support or proper armrests; poorly designed computer tables or study desks without proper slant and height; sofas without proper consistency, firmness, height, and back support.
- **Constriction.** Myofascial pain can result from constriction of the waist muscles due to a tight belt, chest muscle constriction due to a tight brassiere, shoulder muscle constriction due to a heavy professional bag or purse, etc.
- **Nutritional deficiencies.** Myofascial pain can result from deficiencies in Vitamin B1, B6, B12, C, and folic acid.
- **Metabolic and endocrine inadequacies.** Myofascial pain can result from suboptimal thyroid levels or subclinical hypothy-

roidism, low glucose levels, high uric acid levels, and iron deficiency or anemia.

- **Medication.** Various medications can contribute to myofascial pain, such as cytotoxic drugs, anti-hypertension drugs, and lithium.
- **Infections.** Viral or bacterial allergies can be a contributing factor.
- **Muscle injury.** Stress and injury in your muscle may cause trigger points. Repetitive stress also may increase your risk, like repeated use of a computer.
- **Deconditioned muscles.** Lack of exercise can lead to deconditioning of muscles, which can become prone to the development of myofascial pain and trigger points.
- **General stress and anxiety.** People who frequently experience stress and anxiety may be more likely to develop trigger points in their muscles. One theory holds that these people may be more likely to clench their muscles, a form of repeated strain that leaves muscles susceptible to trigger points. That is why my multi-modality approach emphasizes the lessening and elimination of stress.
- **Age.** Myofascial pain syndrome is more likely in middle-aged adults. It's thought that younger people's muscles better cope with stress and strain, so they aren't as likely to experience the disorder.

Evaluation, Diagnosis, and Treatment

Routine x-rays, EMG, or MRI scans do not provide specific clues to myofascial pain. In addition, pain caused by myofascial trigger points can be aggravated by dry, cold, or humid weather, overuse of certain muscles, and stress, anxiety, or depression. These factors make it difficult to diagnose. The physician's understanding and knowledge of the location, associated patterns of pain, and symptoms and signs produced by each myofascial trigger point are absolutely essential in making a correct diagnosis and effectively treating myofascial pain disorder.

In order to understand the complexity of myofascial pain and how it can be treated through my methods, let's look at one of the disorder's most common manifestations: myofascial headaches.

Myofascial Headaches

Definition: What is a myofascial headache?

Headache is one of the most common pain complaints encountered by healthcare professionals. More than half the patients treated by doctors, emergency rooms, and ambulatory centers are there because of headache symptoms. As a result, millions of work hours are lost daily and millions of employees (between 5% and 10% nationwide) have to take sick leave.

If you have suffered a severe or even a mild headache, you know the helpless, frustrated feeling of being in agony and unable to end the cycle of pain.

Perhaps you could not sit or lie down in any comfortable position because the pain was hitting you so hard from all sides of your head. Your vision was blurry, you felt nauseous, and you ended up vomiting. To make matters worse, your stomach was irritated from consuming fistfuls of analgesics, such as aspirin, Advil, Aleve, or other over-the-counter medications. Consumption of narcotic analgesics and muscle relaxants often make you feel like a zombie. You may forget places you visited or social interactions. A spouse or a lover may misjudge you, call you an excuse monger or accuse you of not wanting to perform intimately. You may be labeled as a drug addict or drug seeker by those near to you, an ordeal that is almost impossible to bear.

On top of it all is the fear of losing your job because of your repeated work absences. Perhaps you made repeated visits to emergency rooms in the middle of the night and received injections of morphine or Demerol or other substances, which soothed your pain only momentarily. Perhaps you went to a headache clinic, with no results. A few days later your ordeal would resume once again.

You've seen fantastic ads on TV about miraculous cures for migraines. This is nothing more than gimmickry from Wall Street and pharmaceutical companies. They make billions from products that are supposedly well-researched and from books written by so-called "professionals." Yet neither the medication nor the books manage to provide pain relief. Meanwhile, students in medical school continue to be trained and conditioned to deliver a diagnosis—migraine headache—that in my opinion and experience simply does not exist.

As a qualified pain specialist, I understand the majority of headaches to be myofascial in nature and not migraines. In fact, I introduced the term myofascial headaches to the general public and to the Library of Congress about ten years ago.

Myofascial headaches are linked to the muscles surrounding the head, neck, shoulders, and upper back muscles. Acute trauma or chronic wear and tear leads to the development of myofascial trigger points in one or many of these muscle groups, often causing not only debilitating headaches but other associated symptoms. These headaches can be unilateral or bilateral; that is to say, on one side of the head or on both.

Each muscle has its distinctive myofascial pain pattern, specific to trigger points in that muscle. For example, if the trigger point is in the shoulder, the pain will be felt in the neck and temple region. This vicious cycle of muscle contraction and myofascial trigger point activity makes these headaches chronic in nature.

Symptoms, Causes, and Risk Factors

Common symptoms include pain in the temples, and the front or back of the head. Symptoms can vary from mild headache, to a feeling of tightness around the head, to throbbing in the temples or a feeling of bursting in the head. Other symptoms include congestion and reddening of the eyes, nose congestion, stiffness in neck and shoulder muscles, dizziness or vertigo-like sensations, occasional postural dizziness (spinning of the head from sudden turning of the head or sitting up from a lying down position or vice versa), blurred vision, nausea and vomiting, sensitivity to light, difficulty opening the jaw, and a sensation of blockage in the ears. The involvement of certain neck muscles can sometimes cause the patient to feel that his head is bursting.

Besides headaches, a sudden onset of trigger point activity in the anterior neck muscles has caused drivers to lose control of their cars, leading to serious automobile accidents. In addition, hangovers after alcohol consumption are often the result of trigger point activity in neck muscles.

Myofascial headaches can be short-lived with varying intensity, or may frequently last for months, years, or even one's entire lifetime. Myofascial headaches in children are often dismissed as "growing pains" or an attempt by the child to seek attention. Children who suffer from headaches are often falsely labeled as learning disabled because of their inability to focus and concentrate. This leads to lifelong struggles with low self-esteem, feelings of guilt and inadequacy, and problems with careers and relationships.

Hence, the pain cycle continues unless the patient receives active and appropriate treatment interventions, and complementary or perpetuating factors are eliminated.

Myofascial headaches often result from acute trauma to the head and neck regions (for example, a car accident). More commonly, they are caused by subtle and prolonged wear and tear, atrophy, and deconditioning of neck, shoulder, or upper back muscles. This wear and tear can be the result of a skeletal disproportion, such as a short leg or short hemi pelvis, poor posture (sitting in a poorly designed car seat or chair), bird watching, or ill-fitting glasses. Myofascial headaches can also be caused by psychological stressors, anxiety, and depression, repetitive trauma to neck and shoulder muscles caused by computer use, exposure to extreme temperatures, and hypothyroidism (clinical or sub-clinical).

The neck muscles are a frequent and vastly overlooked cause of headaches. Patients are mistakenly diagnosed with migraine headaches and treated unsuccessfully with long lists of pain and migraine medications. Frequently, on careful examination, this patient's pain originates from trigger points in the temple, occiput, neck, shoulder, or upper back muscles, and is not merely the result of vasodilation or vasoconstriction of intracranial vessels, the purported cause of so-called migraines. Any agent, such as an anti-migraine pill or spray, can surely produce placebo effects of temporary analgesia, but will not the cure the true underlying causes or aetiology.

Evaluation, Diagnosis, and Treatment

Migraine is a French word, which means one-sided headache. However, this term has been used by doctors and laymen alike—incorrectly—to describe many different types of pain in the head and neck area. Most headaches are misdiagnosed as migraines. According to recent studies, more than 90% of headaches are myofascial in nature and only about 6% are migraines.

Traditional diagnostic methods, such as MRI or CT scans, EEG, and X-rays, often fail to identify the underlying cause, namely, the myofascial trigger points producing these headaches.

When I started treating spreading the gospel of multimodality pain management 25 years ago, both the general public and medical professionals often wondered, to put it frankly, what the hell I was talking about. They often questioned where I was coming from and my rationale. They felt puzzled that all they had read or heard did not quite match what I was saying. So they were skeptical when I said migraines do not exist. They remained skeptical until I began producing results by treating patients with shots in the head, neck, shoulders, and upper back.

In addition, I started employing preventive measures, such as proper use and consistency of pillows during sleep, protecting the neck and shoulder muscles against cold drafts at night during winter or summer months, daily exercises of neck muscles, and correction of skeletal disproportion (i.e. short legs or short hemi-pelvis, short arms, and rounded shoulders, which could precipitate headaches repeatedly if uncorrected by measures like heel and butt lifts, as well as a chair with adjustable side arms.). In addition, I advocate proper posture and use of ergonomically designed furniture with proper back support. Excessive computer use and poor arm support often lead to an overloading of neck, shoulder, and arm muscles, which often leads to two common pain disorders, myofascial headaches and so-called carpel tunnel syndrome. In addition, patients can suffer from pins and needles and numbness in particular areas of their hands due to cervical nerve entrapment (entrapment neuropathy) in the neck muscles.

Despite the failure of traditional methods, myofascial headaches respond very well to treatment. With appropriate treatment, I have dispelled many myths about the diagnosis and treatment of migraines. My pain management techniques offer the promise of long-lasting headache relief and even complete cure.

Treatment begins with a thorough evaluation and appropriate diagnosis. Once the diagnosis has been made, I design a treatment plan that includes multi-modality therapies.

The most important modality is injections into the trigger points, leading to deactivation of trigger points and spinal reflex, which allows muscles to regain their normal flexibility and range of motion. Therapeutic exercises, including stretching and strengthening of the affected muscles, also play a significant role in healing. In addition, narcotic and non-narcotic pain medication, as well as antidepressants, are prescribed, and are reinforced by meditation therapy and psychotherapy if necessary. Elimination or correction of complementary factors, such as short leg, hypothyroidism, or poorly designed furniture, is very essential. The patient's active participation, cooperation, and compliance, including follow-up treatments and visits, are absolutely essential for a favorable treatment outcome.

Parallel with these treatment modalities, I introduce measures to deal with factors that perpetuate the pain or may have triggered it in the first place. One example would be to correct the inequality in length in the patient's legs.

Ergonomics, the science of designing workplace equipment to fit the worker and prevent repetitive strain injuries, may also play a role in the treatment or even prevention of myofascial pain. For example, for a person sitting all day in front of a computer, a properly designed computer chair is essential, as well as use of an appropriate-sized pillow or pillows with right consistency (usually medium foam) for sleep.

All these treatments, in combination, can heal and prevent myofascial headaches. I have often told patients, "Your diagnosis is myofascial headache, not migraines, and I shall prove it to you sooner than later, perhaps on your next visit when I start treating you."

Often the first treatment brings the much desired and long-awaited results, which are maintained by follow up treatments. I have treated hundreds of headache patients successfully and have been called a miracle man.

I am not a miracle man. I am a skilled but humble doctor who understands the true sources of pain and how to treat it effectively. I am dedicated to making this paradigm shift available to the whole of ailing humanity. Ten years ago I submitted my taxonomy of myofascial headache treatment to the Library of Congress.

One of my patients, Ms. KP, had been suffering from migraine headaches for 12 years.

"The pain was so severe I cannot describe it," she says, "but you might imagine how it would feel if someone hammered a sharp nail into your eye and out your temple. The pain affected the entire side of my head, extending down the back of my neck, and even caused me to vomit. To curb the pain my doctor would give me an injection, which only put me to sleep. After each injection it took four days for my body to recover and to function normally again.

"Of course, this affected my family life, my work, and my self-esteem. I averaged two migraine headaches a month. On the last visit to my family doctor, I broke down in tears and said that I could not handle this pain any longer. He recommended that I try the Washington Pain Medicine Center. Since working with Dr. Ajrawat, my life has changed. I never knew that feeling good, felt so good."

Like Ms. KP, my patient Magic suffered from chronic headaches for many years.

In 1997, he started to get blurred vision, headaches, and often felt the need to vomit. He couldn't figure out why this was happening. Over time he saw several doctors and had numerous tests and scans done, but the results always came back negative. He even tried to change his diet, but still found no relief.

Magic finally found a doctor who told him he was experiencing migraines. The doctor recommended daily doses of Inderal. Magic's wife was concerned that taking so much medication might not be a good thing for his long-term health, but her concerns fell on deaf ears.

Finally, in 2008, Magic heard about me and made an appointment.

"Just by looking at me, Dr. Ajrawat told me that I was depressed, and that the headaches that I was experiencing all these years were not migraines but were in fact myofascial headaches," Magic remembers.

"He explained the cause of the headaches and said we were right to be concerned about taking Inderal all these years.

"Without realizing that Inderal was the culprit, I had gained a lot of weight and looked swollen all over. My sugar levels were out of whack. My skin had a yellow undertone. I felt agitated most of the time, and no longer partook in things I used to enjoy, such as weight-lifting, baseball, and hiking. The funny thing is, I didn't realize what was happening to me. Nor did I realize how this was affecting those around me. All I knew was that I was feeling miserable and there was always an underlying unhappiness that I felt. Dr. Ajrawat's consultation started to open my eyes to the fact that something was going on.

"I saw my doctor and started to get off Inderal. Unfortunately, once again, the headaches came back within a few weeks.

"Disappointed, we talked to Dr. Ajrawat about this, and right away he pointed out why I wasn't able to get off the Inderal successfully and live a headache free life. He said I needed to take part in his program in order to slowly get off the medication. My wife and I had never heard of this revolutionary treatment before. Our question was: would it work?

"After doing some research and listening to positive results experienced by Dr. Ajrawat's patients, we decided that it would be well worth the try. What did we have to lose? Things at this point couldn't really get worse for me. I was desperate, but at the same time Dr. Ajrawat made me feel like I would be back to my normal self in no time.

"We decided to take a chance and I went to Washington for treatment. Dr. Ajrawat took so much care and time with me. He was professional and informative. The truly amazing part was that he took a holistic approach and did not treat only my headache pain.

"Today, one and half years after beginning my treatment with Dr. Ajrawat, I am both headache and medication free. I used to look bloated, but now that has disappeared. I have lost thirty pounds and feel alive again. My depression has lifted, I'm playing sports, and I look forward to doing things. People say that I have color in my face again. These are just some of the positive things that have occurred.

"Dr. Ajrawat's incredible treatment has truly saved my life. He reversed 13 years of pain and suffering."

Neck, Back, and Shoulder Pain

Definition: What is neck, back, and shoulder pain?

Back and shoulder pain are very common ailments. Most people in the U.S. will experience them at some point.

In addition, neck muscles can be strained by poor posture, when either standing or sitting. Wear and tear can also lead to neck pain.

As anyone who has had neck pain knows, it can be a debilitating condition that affects every aspect of your life.

On a positive note, my pain management techniques can largely eliminate or prevent most episodes of back, neck, and shoulder pain, usually within a few weeks. Using my techniques, surgery is rarely needed to treat it.

Symptoms, Causes, and Risk Factors

Symptoms of back pain may include aching, shooting, or stabbing pain in the lower back, often radiating down your lower leg. Other symptoms include a limited range of motion and difficulty in maintaining an erect posture.

Acute back pain may last a few weeks, while chronic back pain lasts for three months or longer.

A complicated structure of bones, muscles, ligaments, tendons, and disks forms the back. Back pain can arise from problems with any of these component parts, such as a ruptured or bulging disk that presses on a nerve, but myofascial pain is the major cause of neck, back, shoulder, and knee pain. Skeletal disproportion (having long second metatarsal bones or rounded shoulders) or irregularities, constriction of muscles by tight belts, and/or prolonged immobility can lead to myofascial back pain. However, it most often occurs when an awkward movement or heavy lifting strains muscles and ligaments. This pain can be accompanied by muscle spasms.

Factors that can increase the risk of developing back pain include obesity, physically strenuous work, repetitive trauma, stress, anxiety, and depression.

Symptoms of neck pain include shooting pain into your shoulder or down your arm, numbness or loss of strength in your arms or hands, and an inability to touch your chin to your chest

Neck pain can result from overuse, poor posture, injuries, whiplash injuries that are common in auto accidents, and activation of myofascial trigger points. Diseases are also a contributing factor, such as rheumatoid arthritis and meningitis.

You can injure your neck by spending hours hunched over a computer. Neck muscles can become fatigued and eventually strained when you overuse your neck muscles repeatedly, leading to the development of myofascial trigger points that cause chronic pain. The neck is easily injured by simple instances of poor posture, such as reading in bed without the proper support. Osteoarthritis in your neck can develop from normal wear and tear along with the rigors of aging. In addition, the nerves in the neck can become compressed by stiffened muscles or herniated disks and bone spurs.

Risk factors for neck pain include age and occupation or a certain posture (if your job requires your neck to be held in one position for prolonged periods of time, such as when driving or doing computer work).

Evaluation, Diagnosis, and Treatment

Starting in 2005, Mr. JB began to notice disturbing changes in the way his body functioned. He would get up four or five times a night to use the bathroom, only to find out he really didn't need to go. He didn't sleep very well and, when he did, would grind his teeth because of the pain he felt in various parts of his body. His arm and leg muscles started getting weaker.

JB grew depressed. He suffered with constant back pain, which radiated into his neck and shoulders. Tremors in both hands made the simplest tasks difficult to accomplish.

JB came to my pain center, where I examined him and made a diagnosis. "When I first visited," he recalls, "I was weak and couldn't hold my legs up for more than a short time. I had extreme pain in both shoulders and my back bothered me as well."

Mr. JB was started on a treatment schedule, where I used a combination of approaches to manage and eliminate his pain, including trigger point injections, Ajrawat Air-Pulse Autonomic Therapy, stretching and strengthening exercises, physical therapy, hot packs, and electric stimulation. These approaches in combination have significantly reduced JB's pain.

"My right shoulder now is 90% better," JB says. "My legs are much stronger than before. My back is a lot stronger than before. My left shoulder has improved but still needs additional treatments. All in all, I find my treatment results so far to be amazing."

My wife, a board-certified psychiatrist, treated JB for his depression and other issues. With medication and psychotherapy, she brought new balance to JB's life.

"This has been a long difficult journey that has brought me new hope for brighter times," he says. "When you have suffered for so long, it's hard to believe in something until you actually see it work. I'm 55, and I feel younger and stronger today. I know I will continue to improve and the sky is the limit."

Mr. TC, 42, had been suffering from chronic pain for over 20 years.

A birth defect, a series of accidents, an extremely rare form of viral meningitis (Mollaret's), and the after-effects of two back surgeries combined to make his life a terrifying ordeal. He had gone from one pain clinic after another, hearing the same refrain over and over: "You will be in constant pain for the rest of your life."

"I experienced my first bout of meningitis 21 years ago," TC says. "The doctors didn't know what it was. I almost died. Less than 100 people in the world have been diagnosed with Mollaret's meningitis. I have had more than 30 bouts with it. In 1985 I underwent a spinal fusion to correct offset vertebrae, a birth defect. This was the first of two surgeries on the L4-5 lumbar vertebrae area of my back.

"A couple of years later, I was crushed by a wave at the ocean, dislocating my left shoulder. I had to have a partial claviculectomy. Then in 1994 a car accident crushed part of my L-5 vertebrae, which became fused to my tailbone, and I also suffered a sprained neck. I had a second surgery on the L-5 area of my back nine months later. Even though the surgeon was able to remove the broken pieces of vertebrae, he warned me that scar tissue entangling with nerves could become a problem.

"Several months after the second operation I began having pain at the site of the surgery, as well as in my legs and feet. I was prescribed steroid shots, anti-inflammatory medicine, trigger point injections, epidural nerve blocks, a Transcutaneous Electrical Nerve Stimulator (TENS) unit, heat packs, and physical therapy—none of which worked. It was suggested that I try acupuncture, which I did. That didn't help, either. After having tried everything recommended, to no avail, my doctor said I should try a pain clinic because he knew of no other course of action.

"I put off going to a pain clinic as long as I could—about two years. Finally, in 1999, my pain problem had become so extreme that my fiancée persuaded me to try a pain clinic because it seemed to her there was no other place to seek help.

"The first pain clinic I went to prescribed physiotherapy and one Percocet a day. After several months of this therapy not working I switched to another pain clinic. My new pain specialist prescribed 30 mg. of Oxycontin per day. As I adjusted to the medication, the dosage would be increased. At this point I was forced to change pain clinics by my insurance company. My new pain clinic continued my current pain medication therapy. They also suggested I try a course of epiduralysis, which I did. The five treatments of epiduralysis did not help, as manifested by the fact that, over a two year period, my Oxycontin dose had to be gradually increased to 260 mg. a day. At that time my pain specialist lost his license, forcing me to look for yet another pain clinic. The anxiety I was experiencing from not being able to complete the epiduralysis treatment (which was my only hope of getting out of pain at that time), combined with stress from finding a new pain clinic, was enough to cause panic attacks.

"My new pain specialist prescribed Valium for anxiety, Ambien to help me sleep, and Oxycontin for pain. I was taking 260 mg. of Oxycontin, 30 mg. of Valium, and 20 mg. of Ambien per day. Despite the Ambien, adverse reaction to Oxycontin kept me awake for days at a time. I had reached the point where the medication that was supposed to help me caused as much discomfort as I would have experienced if I had not been taking any medication and just suffered with the pain.

"The quality of my life was now at an all point low. Ever since the first surgery, the back pain has interfered with my sleep and exacerbated the pain in my left shoulder. In fact, sleeping was darn near impossible. All this was occurring at the same time the country was attacked on September 11, 2001. Misery is the only word that can describe how I felt. I was afraid to drive a car because I wasn't sure of myself. I couldn't concentrate on the things that usually came naturally to me. I would lie in bed sometimes for days, unable to sleep but so exhausted that I couldn't get up. My life revolved around taking my next Oxycontin pill and whether I had enough energy to make it to my next appointment with the pain specialist.

"By now I had been told by four different pain clinics and two neurosurgeons that I would be in permanent chronic pain from scar tissue wrapping around nerves at the site of the two operations. I requested that I be taken off all medications because the side effects were now worse than being in pain itself. The pain specialist refused. He insisted that if I went off the medications, I would be right back on them in less than one month."

At this point, TC found about my Washington Pain Medicine Center. He called to see if we might offer a treatment different from the other pain clinics he had visited. Our approach sounded different to TC, so he called and scheduled an appointment.

"During my first appointment with Dr. P.S. Ajrawat, he pointed out some fundamental problems with my body that other doctors either missed or didn't think were important. I was impressed with his all-inclusive examination. He was the first doctor who said I would not have to live in permanent pain. I was skeptical because of what other doctors had told me, but I wanted off of the pain medication so badly that I hoped and prayed what he said was true.

"My first appointment was on November 28, 2001. I took my last Oxycontin pill on December 17, 2001, a date I will never forget. Dr. Ajrawat began treating me with trigger point injections that were very different from the trigger point injections I had previously received. The injections were mostly into the muscles surrounding the site of my operations. The treatments Dr. Ajrawat gave me provided pain relief almost immediately. In group therapy, I learned how vital an all-inclusive program is to the recovery of pain patients. It was also helpful to talk to other people with problems similar to mine. Another important part of the treatment plan included an exercise program specifically designed to my recovery needs. I was also encouraged to do stretching and strengthening exercises and walk regularly at home."

TC's other health problems diminished as well. Since 1983, he had been hospitalized 30 times for episodes of viral meningitis. On average, he was getting sick once or twice a year. During his two years of treatment at WPMC, TC was sick only once.

"Over the two-year course of seeing Dr. Ajrawat for treatments, the pain I had been suffering from has nearly disappeared. The number of shots I require has declined from two sets of injections a week to one set of shots per week, and sometimes even less frequently. I'm an accomplished guitar player and, not being hindered by constant pain, I am able once again to concentrate and be creative.

"What I'm really trying to say here is that WPMC treats the whole of you, everything—your psychological as well as physical problems. I believe this is one of the key elements in my successful rehabilitation and the relief of my severe back, shoulder, and neck pain.

"Dr. Ajrawat's dynamic, multi-modality model seems to have changed virtually every aspect of my life—emotionally, physically, and spiritually. My endurance level has increased so dramatically that I feel stronger and healthier than at any time in the past 10 years."

Kenneth is yet another patient who came to me suffering from lower back pain.

"Historically I have been a somewhat athletic person and was a competitive runner. After my car accident, I experienced constant back, leg, and nerve pain continuously, and conventional treatment offered little relief. I became addicted to prescription medication and, with little activity, gained over 70 pounds. I required canes in order to walk and became very depressed.

"I had the good fortune to find Dr. Paramjit Singh Ajrawat, and by following his treatment plan, my pain subsided. I became physically active once again, lost all of the excess weight I gained, and my depression went away. Today, I am once again fully productive."

Knee Pain

Definition: What is Knee Pain?

Nearly a third of Americans over 45 report some episodes of knee pain. While not all knee pain is serious, some forms of it can lead to increasing pain, joint damage , and even disability if left untreated.

I have had great success treating knee pain with my multimodality treatment methods. Sometimes a ruptured ligament or tendon may require surgical repair, but in the vast majority of my cases I have healed knee pain without the patient resorting to surgery.

Although every knee problem can't be prevented (especially if you're active), I train my patients in healthful ways of living that can reduce the risk of injury or re-injury.

Symptoms, Causes, and Risk Factors

A ruptured ligament or torn cartilage can cause knee pain, as well as certain medical conditions, including arthritis, gout, and infection. But the most common cause of knee pain is myofascial trigger points in the muscles adjoining to the knee. These include the muscles on the front, back, and sides of the knee joint. The signs and symptoms of knee problems can vary widely because of the knee's complexity, the number of structures involved, the amount of use it gets over a lifetime, and the range of injuries and diseases that can cause knee pain. Joints are very complex parts of the body, which allow flexibility, support, and a wide range of motion.

Your knees are hinge joints, which, as the name suggests, work much like the hinge of a door, allowing the joint to move backward and forward. The knee is the largest, heaviest, and most complex hinge joint in the body. In addition to bending and straightening, they twist and rotate. This makes them especially vulnerable to damage, which is why they sustain more injuries on average than do other joints. Ligaments, tendons, cartilage, and bursae (fluid-filled sacs surrounding the knee) are all vulnerable to damage and disease.

Knee injuries are usually caused by a blow to the knee, repeated stress or overuse, or sudden and awkward movements, such as during sports. Degeneration from aging is also a factor. But myofascial trigger points resulting from skeletal disproportion, such as leg length inequality, are indeed the common cause of knee, back, and shoulder pain.

Your chances of suffering knee pain are exacerbated by being overweight or obese, or by repetitive activity that can stress the knee by weakening muscles around the joint. In addition, knee injuries can be caused by a lack of strength and flexibility.

Another major factor that is overlooked by traditional practitioners but that I address is my practice is structural abnormalities, such as having one leg shorter than the other, misaligned knees, and even flat feet.

Evaluation, Diagnosis, and Treatment

Marcia is an example of my successful treatment of knee pain. A number of years ago she was severely injured in an accident. As a pedestrian, she was crushed between two vehicles. The impact was so great she thought she had died. Her left leg was twisted at a severe angle.

She was rushed to the hospital, where doctors drilled into her left calf bone and inserted a rod. Marcia was in traction for three months. The doctors told her she might lose her left leg; if she kept the leg, it would take a year to walk. Nevertheless, Marcia was back at work the following July with her leg in a cast brace.

Still, Marcia was in constant pain. She suffered from nerve damage in both legs. Her injured leg was now shorter and crooked, and she walked with a cane. Even narcotic pain relievers offered no help.

"I tried everything—water exercise which increased my mobility, acupuncture which increased my strength, pain medication which helped me sleep two to three hours a day. And physical therapy kept me moving. With no ability for vigorous physical activity, I gained a lot of weight, going from 136 to 240 pounds. I also had both knees replaced. By this time I had gone from morphine to a fentanyl patch to control my pain.

"Upon meeting and talking to Dr. Ajrawat at our first consultation, I found him very personable and approachable. After many years of doctors, disappointments, and pain, this sense of connection and caring was very important to me.

"His treatments included nerve blocks, trigger point injections, physical rehabilitation, exercises, and Ajrawat Air-Pulse Autonomic Therapy. I now have days of pain relief and only use pain relievers sporadically. I can pull weeds from my garden. I can pray on my knees. His exercises have strengthened my legs and arms, giving me better balance and stamina. My weight has dropped to 213. I have also stopped smoking, a habit that picked up after the fentanyl patch didn't help relieve my nerve pain. Dr. Ajrawat has been a miracle in my life."

Pelvic pain

Definition: What is pelvic pain?

Chronic pelvic pain refers to pain in your pelvic region that lasts six months or longer. While it can be a disorder in its own right, it can also be a symptom of another disease.

The cause of chronic pelvic pain is often hard to diagnose, particularly with traditional treatment methods. Numerous patients who have come to me complaining of pelvic pain have never received a specific diagnosis explaining their pain. But that doesn't mean their pain isn't real and treatable.

My treatment methods focus on the causes of pelvic pain and managing the resulting pain and discomfort.

Symptoms, Causes, and Risk Factors

Symptoms of chronic pelvic pain include pressure or heaviness deep within the pelvis. The pain can be severe, intermittent, or dull. You may also experience pain during intercourse, a bowel movement, or when you sit down.

If you have to stand for long periods of time, your discomfort may intensify. You may find that you have to miss work, can't sleep, and can't exercise.

Pelvic pain can commonly result from myofascial trigger points in the inner thigh muscles and pelvic floor muscles, as well as from menstrual cramps, rupture of an ectopic pregnancy, ovarian cyst, or other mass, endometriosis, and pelvic inflammatory disease. In my experience, myofascial pain arising from myofascial trigger points in the buttock muscles, pelvic floor muscles, and inner thigh muscles are one of the common causes of pelvic pain, often leading to unnecessary procedures such as laprascopic examination or surgeries. Non-gynecologic causes of pelvic pain can include urinary tract infections, intestinal obstruction, colitis, tumors, and appendicitis.

Evaluation, Diagnosis, and Treatment

As we saw in Chapter One, Sandra was suffering from myofascial pain confined to her lower back, pelvic area, and right upper and inner thigh area, which was causing her both local and referred pain. This led to pelvic pain, the causes of which were misdiagnosed before she consulted me. In addition, Sandra had a skeletal disproportion—her short leg perpetuated her pelvic pain. Finally, her anxiety, depression, and anger after her son's murder heightened the intensity of her physical pain, which in turn fueled her anxiety and depression in a vicious cycle.

In short, Sandra's pelvic pain was a classic example of the complexity and multi-dimensionality of pain. Sandra's pain was alleviated by nerve blocks, trigger point injections, physical therapy, strengthening and stretching exercises, pain medication, and, most importantly, Ajrawat Air-Pulse Autonomic Therapy.

Kate, who we also met in the first chapter, suffered from pelvic pain due to severe menstrual cramps. Her pain was not restricted to abdominal or pelvic pain—she got cramps in her upper legs and lower back as well.

"These severe cramps started when I was 17. I would take several 800 mg. doses of Ibuprofen throughout the day to just get by, but the medication barely touched the pain. It only made it bearable to get through school so I could get home and nap, which happened rarely because I was an active high school student.

"When I was 20, I began to take combination hormonal birth control pills. These helped somewhat. They mostly helped in reducing my flow and shortening the duration of menstruation. However, I was still plagued by cramps. I had consulted with my various doctors over the years. Ibuprofen, heating pads, and long baths were common suggestions, but I was repeatedly told that each woman's cycle was different. Doctors said I happened to be the one unfortunate individual who had to deal with more discomfort than most.

"So when I mentioned the pain to Dr. Ajrawat, he said I may have certain muscle trigger points in my abdomen and legs that could lead to the painful cramping. He began to work on those trigger points. My first trigger point treatment in the abdominal area revealed many other trigger points. When I started my next menstrual cycle, I noticed a marked decrease in pelvic pain, as well as the pain in my quads that had plagued me for so long. I was so grateful Dr. Ajrawat took my pain seriously. He explained that after repeated trigger point treatments I should experience even more relief. It's such a blessing I experience less cramping. I really believe Dr. Ajrawat's holistic approach to pain has benefited me in so many ways.

"Too often women think or are told that menstrual pain is just part of the monthly process. However, if you experience the kind of pain that I did, do not be afraid to speak up. Your body is telling you something is out of balance. Dr. Ajrawat's treatments continue to bring my body and mind back into balance. For that, I will be eternally grateful."

Cancer pain

Definition: What is cancer pain?

About a third of people with cancer experience cancer pain. Your chances of experiencing such pain are higher if you have cancer that has spread or recurred.

Symptoms, Causes, and Risk Factors

Cancer pain can range across the spectrum, from severe to intermittent to mild. Cancer pain can come from the primary cancer itself (where the cancer started) or from areas in the body where the cancer has spread. As a tumor grows, it may put pressure on nerves, bones, or other organs, causing pain. Cancer pain may be also due to chemicals the cancer secretes in the region of the tumor. Treatment of the cancer can help the pain in these situations.

Cancer treatments, such as chemotherapy, radiation, and surgery, are another source of pain. Radiation may create a burning sensation or painful scars, while chemotherapy can result in mouth sores, diarrhea, and nerve damage.

Evaluation, Diagnosis, and Treatment

Jimmie, 67 years old, suffered from severe pain in his legs and feet in the two years before he saw me.

"I experienced my first bout of nerve damage two years ago after having chemo treatments for bladder cancer. I have been seen by two neurologists, have had several nerve studies conducted, and have been prescribed a variety of drugs that didn't work. I lived in pain 24 hours a day and couldn't sleep more than a couple of hours a night. I was starting to become depressed."

Jimmie was referred to me in 2009. I diagnosed his peripheral neuropathy and began treating him with sympathetic nerve blocks, trigger point injections, and heat treatments, along with physical rehabilitation and exercise and Ajrawat Air-Pulse Autonomic Therapy. After the first series of injections Jimmie was walking without pain in his legs.

"Though I had been retired and disabled, I have now started working part time, 22 hours a week. I feel happy and good again."

Diabetic Neuropathy

Definition: What is diabetic neuropathy?

Diabetic neuropathy is a disorder of the nerves caused by high levels of sugars in the blood. For people with diabetes, this condition can, over time, develop into nerve and tissue damage throughout the body, including the peripheral nerves, the heart, the digestive system, the kidneys, and the reproductive system. Different types of diabetic neuropathies exist, including peripheral neuropathy, autonomic neuropathy, proximal neuropathy, and focal neuropathy.

Symptoms, Causes, and Risk Factors

Diabetic neuropathy not only results from high blood sugar levels, but can also be caused by autoimmune deficiency, neurovascular factors (such as ischemia), or decreased blood supply to the nerves. Complementary factors, such as smoking, alcohol use, and medications, can precipitate the condition. Symptoms include pain, numbness, burning, and tingling in the toes, feet, legs, arms, hands, and fingertips.

In addition, other common symptoms include diarrhea, constipation, indigestion, weakness, dizziness, insomnia, depression, anxiety, weight loss, problems with urination (urinary incontinence or loss of bladder control), erectile dysfunction, impotence, vision change, fasciculation, muscle weakness, and difficulty standing, walking, or bearing weight.

Evaluation, Diagnosis, and Treatment

Until now, diabetic neuropathy treatment has been oriented toward pain relief through the use of conventional approaches, such as the use of medications like gabapentin, exercise, and other adjunctive treatment measures, but these approaches have not been effective in treating it.

Departing from traditional methods, I have achieved great success in treating diabetic neuropathy with a combination of sympathetic nerve blocks, trigger point injections, antidepressants, and narcotic and non-narcotic analgesics. My approach to treating diabetic neuropathy is based on increasing blood supply to the nerves through the use of sympathetic nerve blocks and daily use of scientific meditation therapy. Through Bi-Directional Psychosomatic Autonomic Feedback, meditation therapy reverses damage done to the nerves caused by ischemia and restores circulation by establishing a balance between the sympathetic and parasympathetic components of the autonomic nervous system. It also helps normalize the levels of various neurotransmitters, such as serotonin, nor-epinephrine, acetylcholine, dopamine, and glutamate, among others.

Regular use of sympathetic nerve blocks, Autonomic Therapy, antidepressants, analgesics, physical rehabilitation, and psychotherapy has led to incredibly positive results. Studies have shown that these approaches not only decrease pain, but also restore lost bodily functions and lower dependence on various anti-diabetic medications, oral as well as parenteral.

Three case histories show the promise and efficacy of my treatments.

When Aaron first came to see me, she suffered from burning feet and was in such great pain that she couldn't even walk. "Pitiful" is the way she described herself. Her little brother had to wheel her into my office in a wheelchair.

"I looked a mess because I hadn't had my hair done in three months," Aaron recalled, "and my clothes didn't fit because I had lost a lot of weight. I hadn't slept in almost three months. Can you imagine not sleeping for that long? It wasn't a pretty sight at all."

Aaron's body had shut down because she wasn't taking care of her diabetes.

"Imagine the pain from a Charlie Horse magnified 20 times," she recalls. "Not a good feeling at all. I never thought I would ever get back to normal because I didn't see light at the end of the tunnel. My days got longer and longer, and the pain got worse and worse."

I diagnosed Aaron's condition as diabetic neuropathy and treated her with nerve blocks, trigger point injections, and medication. In addition, she meditated for 20 minutes three or four times a day, exercised regularly, and ate properly. Soon she was able to cut her insulin intake by one third and regained her health.

Walter, 67, started experiencing pain from arthritis in his thirties. He then began suffering from Type-II diabetes. He started taking medication for both conditions.

About 15 years ago, the arthritis spread to Walter's knees and both knees had to be replaced. As a result of the diabetes, he developed neuropathy in both feet.

"The pain was excruciating," Walter recalls. "My feet felt like blocks of wood. Doctors told me that there was nothing they could do. I took pain-killing medicines, such as Oxycodone, Lyrica, Cymbalta, etc. Most of these medications only helped for a few hours and then the pain would start again."

A family member suggested that Walter make an appointment with me.

"The treatments have been like a miracle from God," Walter says. "I no longer have sleepless nights or that killer pain. I can now run, jump, skip, and hop, activities I have not been able to do for about 30 years or more. I truly believe that as time goes by I will improve even more."

Veronica is a final example. She suffered from diabetic neuropathy and chronic myofascial pain in her lower back and extremities. All have been treated successfully after a year under my care.

"The color in my face is back, and my diabetes is getting under control," Veronica says. "I don't have tingling in my fingers anymore. When I first came to Dr. Ajrawat, I thought the pain would never go away, but never say never. I feel very thankful."

Arthritis

Definition: What is arthritis?

Arthritis is a disorder resulting from inflammation of the joints in the body, or the area where two different bones meet. The resulting inflammation leads to joint pain, also known as arthralgia.

Arthritis is the most common chronic illness in the United States. Nearly 40 million people in the United States are affected by it, including over 250,000 children. Approximately 350 million people worldwide have arthritis.

There are over 100 types of arthritis, ranging from those related to cartilage wear (such as osteoarthritis) to those associated with inflammation resulting from an overactive immune system (such as rheumatoid arthritis).

However, most arthritis pain is the result of myofascial trigger points and must be treated in that manner.

Symptoms, Causes, and Risk Factors

Symptoms include pain and limited joint function. Inflammation leads to joint stiffness, swelling, and tenderness. Patients with myofascial trigger points often complain of suddenly falling down while walking as the knee gave out and the patient lost control. Locking and laxity of the knee joint can be commonly seen in patients with torn cartilage or ligaments, which often warrants surgical intervention.

Because they are rheumatic diseases, many forms of arthritis can affect various organs of the body that do not directly involve the joints. Symptoms can include fever, swollen glands, weight loss, fatigue, and even abnormalities in the lungs, heart, or kidneys.

Causes include injury, metabolic abnormalities (such as gout and pseudogout), hereditary factors, and infections.

Evaluation, Diagnosis, and Treatment

As described above, I treat arthritis by treating myofascial trigger points, as described in the section on myofascial pain.

Fibromyalgia

Definition: What is fibromyalgia?

You hurt all over, and you frequently feel exhausted. Even after numerous tests, your doctor can't find anything specifically wrong with you. If this sounds familiar, you may have fibromyalgia.

Fibromyalgia is a chronic condition characterized by widespread pain and stiffness in your muscles, ligaments, tendons, and joints, as well as fatigue and multiple tender points—places on your body where slight pressure causes pain.

Women are much more likely to develop the disorder than are men, and the risk of fibromyalgia increases with age. Fibromyalgia symptoms often begin after a physical or emotional trauma, but in many cases there appears to be no triggering event.

Symptoms, Causes, and Risk factors

Signs and symptoms of fibromyalgia can vary, depending on the weather, stress, physical activity, or even the time of day.

• Widespread pain and tender points

The pain associated with fibromyalgia is described as a constant dull ache, typically arising from muscles. To be considered widespread, the pain must occur on both sides of your body and above and below your waist.

Fibromyalgia is characterized by additional pain when firm pressure is applied to specific areas of your body, called tender points. Tender point locations include the back of the head, between the shoulder blades, top of the shoulders, front sides of neck, upper chest, outer elbows, upper hips, sides of hips, and inner knees.

• Fatigue and sleep disturbances

People with fibromyalgia often awaken tired, even though they seem to get plenty of sleep. Experts believe that these people rarely reach the deep restorative stage of sleep. Sleep disorders that have been linked to fibromyalgia include restless legs syndrome and sleep apnea.

Fibromyalgia is also characterized by anxiety, depression, and disturbances in bowel function. Mental and/or emotional disturbances occur in over half of people with fibromyalgia.

These symptoms include poor concentration, forgetfulness, mood changes, irritability, depression, and anxiety. Since a firm diagnosis of fibromyalgia is difficult, and no confirmatory laboratory tests are available, patients with fibromyalgia are often misdiagnosed as having depression as their primary underlying problem.

Other symptoms of fibromyalgia include tension headaches, numbness or tingling in different parts of the body, abdominal pain related to irritable bowel syndrome ("spastic colon"), and irritable bladder, which causes painful and frequent urination. Like fibromyalgia, irritable bowel syndrome can cause chronic abdominal pain and other bowel disturbances without detectable inflammation of the stomach or the intestines.

Each patient with fibromyalgia is unique. Any of the above symptoms can occur intermittently and in different combinations.

Doctors don't know what causes fibromyalgia, but it most likely involves a variety of factors working together. These may include:

Genetics. Because fibromyalgia tends to run in families, there may be certain genetic mutations that may make you more susceptible to developing the disorder.

Infections. Some illnesses appear to trigger or aggravate fibromyalgia.

Physical or emotional trauma. Post-traumatic stress disorder has been linked to fibromyalgia.

One theory, called central sensitization, states that people with fibromyalgia have a lower threshold for pain because of increased sensitivity in the brain to pain signals.

Researchers believe repeated nerve stimulation causes the brains of people with fibromyalgia to change. This change involves an abnormal increase in levels of certain chemicals in the brain that signal pain, or an increase in neurotransmitters, as we discussed in the previous chapter. In addition, the brain's pain receptors seem to develop a sort of memory of the pain and become more sensitive, meaning they can overreact to pain signals.

The body pain of fibromyalgia can be aggravated by noise, weather changes, and emotional stress.

Risk factors for fibromyalgia include:

Your sex. Fibromyalgia occurs more often in women than in men.

Age. Fibromyalgia tends to develop during early and middle adulthood. But it can also occur in children and older adults.

Disturbed sleep patterns. It's unclear whether sleeping difficulties are a cause or a result of fibromyalgia. But people with sleep disorders, such as nighttime muscle spasms in the legs, restless legs syndrome, or sleep apnea, often have fibromyalgia.

Family history. You may be more likely to develop fibromyalgia if a relative also has the condition.

Rheumatic disease. If you have a rheumatic disease, such as rheumatoid arthritis or lupus, you may be more likely to develop fibromyalgia.

Evaluation, Diagnosis, and Treatment

Patrice was diagnosed with fibromyalgia in 2003. Her first pain management physician prescribed Oxycontin (10mg.), Oxycodone (20mg.), and a regimen of physical therapy at a local rehabilitation hospital. Although the medication and physical therapy helped somewhat, it did not markedly improve her fibromyalgia. Moreover, Patrice did not want to become dependent upon the medication.

Her physician then chose to prescribe Lyrica in addition to the medication she was already taking. The side effects caused her ankles and feet to swell, and she gained 40 pounds. Despite being medicated, her chronic pain did not dissipate. When Patrice's fibromyalgia was particularly severe, she went to the emergency room for treatment, which resulted in more pain medicine and muscle relaxant prescriptions.

Then Patrice contacted me.

"During my initial evaluation," she says, "I learned that one leg was shorter than the other and Dr. Ajrawat was kind enough to present me with shoe inserts in order to equal out my balance. I was started on multimodality treatments, which included trigger point injections, nerve blocks, physical rehabilitation, meditation therapy, medications, and psychotherapy with Dr. S. K. Ajrawat. I learned I had previously thought that exercise would exacerbate my pain and not help treat it, but Dr. Ajrawat taught me how exercise plays an important role in chronic pain management. I also learned how to meditate, and through this technique I have broken a 28-year smoking habit."

Irritable Bowel Syndrome

Definition: What is irritable bowel syndrome?

Irritable bowel syndrome (IBS) is a common disorder that affects the large intestine (colon) and commonly causes cramping, abdominal pain, bloating, gas, diarrhea, and constipation. Fortunately, IBS doesn't cause inflammation or changes in bowel tissue or increase your risk of colorectal cancer. About 20% of Americans experience the condition. I have treated it successfully through multiple modalities, including changes in diet, lifestyle, and stress.

Symptoms, Causes, and Risk Factors

The signs and symptoms of irritable bowel syndrome can vary widely from person to person and often resemble those of other diseases, which complicates accurate diagnosis. Common symptoms are cramping, abdominal pain, bloating, gas, diarrhea, and constipation.

The causes of irritable bowel syndrome are not always clear. The walls of the intestines are lined with layers of muscle that contract and relax in a coordinated rhythm as they move food from your stomach and through your intestinal tract. If you have irritable bowel syndrome, the contractions may be stronger and last longer than normal. Food is forced through your intestines more quickly, causing gas, bloating, and diarrhea.

Abnormalities in your nervous system or colon also may play a role, causing you to experience greater than normal discomfort when your abdomen stretches from gas.

Triggers for IBS can range from gas or pressure on your intestines to certain foods, medications, or emotions.

Many people have occasional signs and symptoms of irritable bowel syndrome, but you're more likely to have IBS if you are young, female, and have a history of IBS.

The effects of IBS may cause you to feel you're not living life to the fullest, leading to discouragement or even depression.

Hypertension or High Blood Pressure

Definition: What is high blood pressure?

High blood pressure (HBP) or hypertension means high pressure (tension) in the arteries. Arteries are the vessels that carry blood from the pumping heart to all the tissues and organs of the body. High blood pressure does not mean excessive emotional tension, although emotional tension and stress can temporarily increase blood pressure.

Normal blood pressure is below 120/80; blood pressure between 120/80 and 139/89 is called "pre-hypertension", and a blood pressure of 140/90 or above is considered high. The top number, the systolic blood pressure, corresponds to the pressure in the arteries as the heart contracts and pumps blood forward into the arteries. The bottom number, the diastolic pressure, represents the pressure in the arteries as the heart relaxes after the contraction. The diastolic pressure reflects the lowest pressure to which the arteries are exposed.

An elevation in blood pressure increases the risk of developing heart disease, kidney disease, hardening of the arteries (atherosclerosis or arteriosclerosis), eye damage, and stroke. For that reason, the diagnosis of high blood pressure is important so efforts can be made to normalize blood pressure and prevent complications.

The American Heart Association estimates high blood pressure affects approximately one in three adults in the United States, or 73 million people.

Symptoms, Causes, and Risk Factors

There are two forms of high blood pressure: essential (or primary) hypertension and secondary hypertension. Essential hypertension is a far more common condition and accounts for 95% of hypertension. Several combined factors produce essential hypertension. In secondary hypertension, which accounts for 5% of hypertension, the high blood pressure is caused by a specific abnormality in one of the organs or systems of the body.

Essential hypertension affects approximately 72 million Americans, yet its basic causes are not always known. Some facts, however, are clear. For example, essential hypertension develops only in groups or societies that have a fairly high intake of salt, exceeding 5.8 grams daily. Approximately 30% of cases of essential hypertension are attributable to genetic factors. For example, in the United States, the incidence of high blood pressure is greater among African Americans than among Caucasians or Asians. Also, in individuals who have one or two parents with hypertension, high blood pressure is twice as common as in the general population.

The vast majority of patients with essential hypertension have in common a particular abnormality of the arteries: an increased resistance (stiffness or lack of elasticity) in the tiny arteries that are most distant from the heart (peripheral arteries or arterioles). Just what makes the peripheral arteries become stiff is not known. Yet, this increased peripheral arteriolar stiffness is present in those individuals whose essential hypertension is associated with genetic factors, obesity, lack of exercise, overuse of salt, and aging.

Inflammation also may play a role in hypertension since a predictor of the development of hypertension is the presence of an elevated C reactive protein level (a blood test marker of inflammation) in some individuals.

Uncomplicated high blood pressure usually occurs without any symptoms (silently) and so hypertension has been labeled "the silent killer." Some people with uncomplicated hypertension, however, may experience symptoms such as headache, dizziness, shortness of breath, and blurred vision.

Substance abuse and addiction

Definition: What is substance abuse and addiction?

People abuse drugs, alcohol, and tobacco for varied and complicated reasons, but in the end our society pays a huge cost in money, lost lives, and criminal behavior.

Addiction is a chronic, often relapsing brain disease that causes compulsive drug use despite harmful consequences to the individual. One very common belief is that drug abusers should be able to just stop taking drugs if they are only willing to change their behavior.

However, drug addiction is a brain disease because the abuse changes the structure and function of the brain. Over time these changes affect a person's self control and ability to make sound decisions, and at the same time create an intense craving to take drugs.

It is because of these changes in the brain that it is so challenging for a person who is addicted to stop abusing drugs. Fortunately, by combining Ajrawat Air-Pulse Autonomic Therapy with other treatments like psychotherapy and medication, individuals can counteract the disruptive effects of addiction and gain control.

Symptoms, Causes, and Risk Factors

Signs of drug abuse include abandonment of past activities, declining grades, changes in mood and behavior, lying, taking risks, and avoiding friends or family in order to get drunk or high.

Drugs are chemicals that tap into the brain's communication system and disrupt the way nerve cells normally send, receive, and process information. There are at least two ways that drugs are able to do this: (1) by imitating the brain's natural chemical messengers, and/or (2) by overstimulating the "reward circuit" of the brain.

Some drugs, such as marijuana and heroin, have a similar structure to the chemical messengers, or neurotransmitters, which are naturally produced by the brain. Because of this similarity, these drugs are able to "fool" the brain's receptors and activate nerve cells to send abnormal messages.

Other drugs, such as cocaine or methamphetamine, can cause the nerve cells to release abnormally large amounts of natural neurotransmitters, or prevent the normal recycling of these brain chemicals, which is needed to shut off the signal between neurons. This disruption produces a greatly amplified message that ultimately disrupts normal communication patterns.

Nearly all drugs, directly or indirectly, target the brain's reward system by flooding the circuit with dopamine. Dopamine is a neurotransmitter present in regions of the brain that control movement, emotion, motivation, and feelings of pleasure. The overstimulation of this system, which normally responds to natural behaviors that are linked to survival (eating, spending time with loved ones, etc), produces euphoric effects in response to the drugs. This reaction sets in motion a pattern that "teaches" people to repeat the behavior of abusing drugs.

As a person continues to abuse drugs, the brain adapts to the overwhelming surges in dopamine by producing less dopamine or by reducing the number of dopamine receptors in the reward circuit. As a result, dopamine's impact on the reward circuit is lessened, reducing the abuser's ability to enjoy the drugs and the things that previously brought pleasure. This decrease compels those addicted to drugs to keep abusing drugs in order to attempt to bring their dopamine function back to normal. And, they may now require larger amounts of the drug than they first did to achieve the dopamine high—an effect known as tolerance.

Certain risk factors may increase someone's likelihood to abuse substances, such as a chaotic home environment or lack of nurturing and parental attachment, poor social coping skills, poor school performance, and perception of approval of drug use behavior

Yet no single factor can predict whether or not a person will become addicted to drugs. Risk for addiction is influenced by a person's biology, social environment, and age or stage of development.

Frozen shoulder

Definition: What is frozen shoulder?

Frozen shoulder is characterized by stiffness, limitation of range of motion, and pain in the shoulder joint, with the patient unable to raise the arm above the shoulder level.

Symptoms, Causes, and Risk Factors

If your arm has been immobilized in a specific position for a prolonged period, such as in a sling for several weeks, you run a greater risk of developing a frozen shoulder.

Evaluation, Diagnosis, and Treatment

Reginald sustained an injury to his right shoulder while showing his son how to do a push up. He heard something rip in the right shoulder and immediately felt a mild ache, which gradually progressed to severe pain over a period of three to four months.

"One day my right shoulder became locked up on me," Reginald recalls. "I could not straighten the arm. From that point onwards, I could lift my right arm only about 40% of its normal range. At this point I went to see my family physician, who prescribed pain pills. This eased the pain somewhat, but I still could not lift my arm. This condition persisted for the next five years. Then, in August 2008, I saw an orthopedic surgeon. He gave me two choices—take pain pills for the rest of my life or get surgery now. So I underwent surgery on my right shoulder for a rotator cuff tear. It helped me for a few months, but after that I could not lift my right arm again for the next two years.

"Then I consulted Dr. Ajrawat. After examining me, he told me that I did not have a rotator cuff tear, but rather myofascial pain that was causing my frozen shoulder. He gave me trigger point injections in the shoulder, after which I was able to raise my arm all the way up without any restrictions. Now I am able to lift my right arm above my head without any pain. I also don't have as much back pain as before. The treatments I have received from Dr. Ajrawat have improved my condition immensely."

Carpal Tunnel Syndrome

Definition: What is carpal tunnel syndrome?

Carpal Tunnel Syndrome (CTS) is associated with pain, numbness, and tingling sensations in the hands, caused by compression of the median nerve, which runs from the forearm into the hand. These symptoms may extend to the shoulder and neck area.

Symptoms, Causes, and Risk Factors

Most cases of Carpal Tunnel Syndrome result from compression of the median nerve in the wrist and hand area. This often results from overextension of the wrist while working on computers, typing, sewing, driving, painting, using tools that vibrate, and work involving fine dexterity. It also can result from narrowing or distortion of the carpal tunnel from rheumatoid arthritis or hypothyroidism. This is commonly an occupational hazard when repetitive trauma is the cause of pain in the wrist and hand, along with a feeling of numbness in the fingers, usually the thumb, first, second, and part of the third finger. In addition, the patient often complains of weakness in the grip, an inability to hold objects, and a sudden proclivity in dropping objects. Myofascial trigger points often accompany the compression of the median nerve and can contribute to or complement the pain.

Evaluation, Diagnosis, and Treatment

Myofascial trigger points in shoulder and arm muscles can refer pain to the wrist, which is commonly misdiagnosed as carpal tunnel syndrome. Diagnostic tests that can diagnose carpal tunnel syndrome include x-rays, EMG (electromyography), and nerve conduction studies.

Decompression of the median nerve using median nerve blocks with local anesthetic solutions is a very effective and conservative treatment. A local anesthetic solution, such as lidocaine 1%, gives instant relief as it expands the carpal tunnel canal and relieves mechanical pressure. This treatment can be repeated as necessary.

Deactivation of the myofascial trigger points can add significantly to pain relief as well, especially when they are complementing or causing the pain in the wrist. Stretching exercises of the wrist, hand, and fingers have been used to combat the pain and numbness caused by repetitive actions.

Piriformis Syndrome

Definition: What is piriformis syndrome?

Piriformis syndrome is a pain disorder that occurs when the sciatic nerve, which stretches from the lower back, through the buttocks, and into the lower legs, is compressed or otherwise irritated by the piriformis muscle. This causes pain, tingling, and numbness in the buttocks and along the path of the sciatic nerve, descending down the lower thigh and into the leg.

Symptoms, Causes, and Risk Factors

Diagnosis is often difficult due to the scarcity of validated and standardized diagnostic tests, but one of the most important criteria is to exclude sciatica resulting from compression/irritation of spinal nerve roots, as by a herniated disk. The syndrome may be due to anatomical variations in the muscle-nerve relationship, or from overuse or strain.

Myofascial trigger points in the piriformis muscle are one of the important causes of piriformis syndrome, as well as radiation of pain down the leg. Skeletal disproportion, like a short lower extremity, can cause myofascial trigger points, which in turn can cause or perpetuate piriformis syndrome on the ipsilateral or contralateral side. Immobility of the sacroliliac joint and hyperpronation of the foot can also cause piriformis syndrome.

A thick wallet carried in the back pocket can cause piriformis syndrome by compressing the nerve or activating myofascial trigger points.

Evaluation, Diagnosis, and Treatment

A detailed patient history and physical examination are key to treatment. Clinical diagnosis can be further aided by diagnostics, like x-rays and MRI scans.

Treatment includes trigger point injections, sacral nerve root blocks, SI joint injections, physical rehabilitation, strengthening and stretching exercises, heel lifts to remedy leg length inequality, analgesics, ergonomically designed chairs or furniture, butt lifts to remedy a short hemipelvis, choosing an alternative site for the wallet, and using good quality shoes with arch supports to prevent hyperpronation of the foot.

Chapter 6

God (Greater Consciousness), Ajrawat Air-Pulse Autonomic Therapy, and the Holy You (Unitary Consciousness)

Having grown up as a Sikh, a religious and God fearing individual, I have always pondered questions of an essential spiritual nature. I have always wondered what kind of supreme force guides our lives, a force which is not visible to our naked eye, and yet whose amazing power we experience and witness every day.

Today mankind ponders, as it has in centuries past, the same spiritual questions.

Yet our ability to ponder and understand our origins becomes even more complex and complicated, as changes in technology continue to advance at the speed of light.

Only a hundred years ago, when the first plane flew at Kitty Hawk, North Carolina for barely 17 seconds, one of the most amazing inventions in the history of mankind awed all of mankind. The world's first airport is in College Park, Maryland, only few miles from my pain center. This is where Wilbur and Orville Wright trained army pilots before and during World War One. Today the airstrip appears no longer than a couple of hundred yards in length. Yet it is not the physical dimensions that make it a monument, but rather the tremendous innovation and pioneering work it represents—the ease of travel the airplane has brought, for the betterment of mankind.

Yet today we take flying for granted, when it once seemed a miracle. Today, a century later, feelings of awe about air travel seem primitive and obsolete. Is it our ingratitude, our indifference, or simply our ease in considering something to be wonderful one instant, and yet outdated and obsolete the next? Have our technological advances jaded us, undermining our capacity for mystery and wonder?

This is a profound question we must ask ourselves. The century that has passed since man's first flight is small in duration, when compared with the sweep of human history. The 20th century marks merely the turn of a single page in the long history of evolution, mankind, and civilization. Despite all our advances, inventions, and technological strides, we still remain uncertain about our biological and spiritual origins, the meaning of our existence, and our relation to the universe.

Is it time to change our frame of reference about spiritual questions and the nature of our existence, without being judgmental about our present belief systems or those of millennia past? I believe the answer is yes.

Though the human mind is evolving every day, and can be very determined, creative, and powerful in dealing with important matters of daily living, it has also repeatedly demonstrated itself to be fragile and vulnerable when it comes to religious conditioning. As pointed out in Chapter Two, this phenomenon is true for practically every religious or belief system. In the domain of religion, the human mind has shown the least introspection, creativity, and analytical ability. Rather, when encountering religion, the human mind shows a surprising (and dangerous) proclivity for being vulnerable to blind, unquestioning conditioning.

This conditioning has been so overwhelming that, today, hundreds of millions of religious followers have become so subservient that they have totally lost their mental and intellectual sovereignty. One can find many examples of this every day by reading the newspaper or watching TV.

In order to reclaim their sovereignty, mental freedom, and sense of empowerment, people must overcome their conditioning, whether it is of a religious, political, or cultural nature. If not, we will only see more conflicts, wars, and destruction for mankind.

It is a monumental task to de-condition the human mind from faulty frames of reference and negative conditioning, and to make it more self-aware, righteous, kind, and loving.

Why is this so? Why have we been unable to change our faulty frames of reference? Because in attempting to do so, we have used the same faulty frames of reference, the same ineffective ways of thinking and processing reality, that caused the problem in the first place—namely, our anecdotal, irrational, conditioned, and unscientific belief systems. To repeat again, in the famous words of Albert Einstein, "A significant problem created at one level of thinking cannot be solved at the same level of thinking."

The great challenge today is to change our approaches towards spirituality and health without being condescending or critical towards previous failed methods and thought processes. Taking such a condescending attitude only creates more problems and conflict. Rather, our challenge is to be open, reasonable, and scientific in our quest to know the ultimate truth. And not only to know that truth, but to practice it in our daily lives.

Despite all the problems posed by religious conditioning, we continue to believe in the possibility—and reality—of a faith backed by just principles: hard work, love for our fellow human beings, the sharing of wealth, forgiveness, a belief in the equality of all mankind, including gender equality, never bowing to oppression no matter how overbearing it might be, never forcing our religious beliefs on others, and, last but not the least, praying for the welfare of all mankind ("Sarbat da Bhalla").

With the great promise offered by my invention of Ajrawat Air-Pulse Autonomic Therapy, along with new research and discoveries by scientists in the fields of medicine and technology, I have come to believe that an amazing force called God or Greater Consciousness does exist. We must try to understand it better and give it our heartfelt gratitude for bringing each of us (or what I call the Unitary Consciousness) into this world as part of its own being. I truly believe we will someday be able to unravel the mystery of our origins. It is always the child's desire to know and see his or her parents. All of mankind has the same desire. I aspire for myself and for everyone to become part of that quest to know ultimate reality, a truth we so desperately need to seek and understand.

As a physician, I know that when two microscopic cells, one male (sperm) and one female (ovum), meet, a new reality is created—the individual or Unitary Consciousness born out of the union of those two microscopic cells. The entire structure of the human mind and body, those parts both visible and invisible, develops via various embryonic stages into a living being with amazing capabilities to create and invent. It is mind boggling to realize that the union of two microscopic cells can produce a human brain capable of storing millions of megabytes of memory as biological binaries. Or that such a human brain can maneuver a spacecraft millions of miles through the solar system to land on other planets. These truths reveal to us that we are indeed a part of that greater reality called God, which has very diligently created every system within our own bodies. We are slowly yet surely discovering this fact for ourselves.

That God (Greater Consciousness or Greater Energy) is out there and also within us is a profound fact in our human reality. As part of that Greater Energy, we too have energy and capabilities within us, both visible and invisible. How we nurture this Unitary Energy or Unitary Consciousness is what will help us unravel the source of our being—the Greater Consciousness or Greater Energy of God.

Neither politics nor mere religious philosophy, as practiced today, will help us reach that goal. One arena is ruled by ego and instant gratification; sacrifice and nobility of purpose guide the other. Yet belief systems, if practiced in traditional ways, will not help us achieve a new kind of awareness or consciousness. By calling ourselves sinners, we condemn the very source we come from. Faulty conditioning of our minds takes us away from ourselves—away from Unitary Consciousness and its source. In contrast, nurturing ourselves and treating ourselves with respect and care will help us understand our origins. By treating ourselves in a holy and respectful manner, we in turn treat our source with respect and reverence.

We honor scientists who do groundbreaking work with awards like the Nobel Prize. But how much scientific effort has gone into discovering how God created human beings? In order to know how we are linked with God or to accept ourselves as being an extension of God, we must keep our minds and bodies balanced, in harmony and in equilibrium. We must take the scientific road to unravel that mystery. Through scientific research throughout the world, we are discovering the complexity of the design of Unitary Consciousness, as created by Greater Consciousness. What is considered science fiction today has often proven to be the factual reality of tomorrow.

My scientific meditation therapy has been a revelation for me on a personal level—it has helped me understand myself better and improved my understanding of human emotions and behaviors. I have also learned how our emotions and behaviors can be improved and maintained with a heart and mind that are both disciplined and open.

But my scientific meditation therapy has also been a revelation on a far larger scale, transcending the mere personal. Ajrawat Air-Pulse Autonomic Therapy can help us achieve a scientific understanding of the Unitary Consciousness, which in turn will lead to our understanding of the great force that originally created us. We already know that great force is responsible for our creation through our own existence, but we have so much more to learn about it.

Playing into the hands of traditional religious dogmatism can only lead us to more faulty conditioning and damaged circuitry in the brain, without ever letting us get closer to ourselves or our origins. Philosophy can be a great source of entertainment and pleasure, but may not show us the path to unifying the Greater Consciousness with Unitary Consciousness. We must acknowledge the need for a scientific basis to our quest—that balanced neurotransmitters, hormones, and normal functioning bring us closer not only to emotional and physical health, but to questions of a deep spiritual nature, to our quest to understand that unitary reality. A negatively conditioned mind and a homeostatically imbalanced body only pose roadblocks to that quest. Our frame of reference must change from a philosophical quest to know God, to a scientific quest that understands the profound relation of a homeostatically balanced mind and body to ultimate questions of spirituality and faith.

I respect and empathize with various religious philosophies that have helped mankind unify with God. But I am a firm believer that the freedom and sanctity of one's own mind must be maintained as well. Without that freedom, we cannot achieve unison with our creator. The ego, narcissism, greed, intimidation, or covert hypnotic tactics of the religious guide or mentor, or, to take the scientific view, the imbalanced neurotransmitters and hormones of the mentor or religious guide, are roadblocks in achieving unison with God. Any faith which is oriented towards the practice of correct principles, and is not based on mere rituals or sheer assumptions, takes us closer to that understanding of

Greater Consciousness, since the correct principles are the product of homeostatically balanced minds and not just fantasy or imagination.

As a Sikh, scientist, and a religious man, I respect all religions and their respective philosophies, as well as all those individuals in the history of mankind who have made their contributions to help humanity. I humbly salute them. In my religion, Sikh Gurus demonstrated by personal sacrifice and martyrdom that correct principles and righteousness must be upheld, as that is the real tribute to our creator and His creation. This has been a great philosophical paradigm and true in many other religions and faiths, and must be respected. Though philosophy gives us great solace and mental peace, it must be complimented by scientific fundamentals and the fervor to know the ultimate truth and to find our way in the ever changing galaxies of time and space. A true revelation of truth comes in accepting the truth and not resisting it.

The time has come when we must use our rational, scientific knowledge to make an all out effort to help those who suffer from pain, stress, and other misfortunes of life. The time is ripe to explore the frontiers of spirituality and health, using innovative and scientific methods to achieve the goals that philosophical concepts and theories have thus far failed to achieve.

The whole idea of enhancing spirituality and health through Ajrawat Air-Pulse Autonomic Therapy is to help individuals achieve mental and physical health and true empowerment of self. My goal is not to enslave them further in the dungeons or black holes of the human ego, but rather to make every individual become mentally and physically at peace with himself, regardless of his race, caste, creed, color, or ethnicity. He will then feel self aware, self assured, loving, kind, self actualized, and at one with him or herself, as the Holy Self (Unitary Consciousness) in harmony and unison with his or her creator, God (Greater Consciousness). This is Autonomic Balance, a state of mental and physical equilibrium achieved with the help of Ajrawat Air-Pulse Autonomic Therapy, through a conscious and disciplined effort.

Our journey through life is very short lived, and we must use everything we possess to make that journey happy, productive, interactive, creative, kind, caring, considerate, giving, principled, and righteous. At the final moment, nothing accompanies us in the casket. The journey of a balanced human, like a star, goes from visible to invisible, from light to dark, and from human to eternal—a never-ending journey or existence. It is a journey made possible through a balanced, self aware, and self realized state, which allows the Unitary Consciousness to merge with the Greater Consciousness

This results in Autonomic Bliss, a state and experience of feeling perfect happiness and joy, after achieving homeostatic balance between mind and body

The final stage is Autonomic Enlightenment, a state of awareness without attachment to worldly objects and passions, a state of contentment and calm in the midst of the galaxies of human neurons and those of the universe, an enlightened state of mind where the darkness of anxiety and self doubt has disappeared.

This harmonious and homeostatically balanced state can be achieved by living in a philosophically righteous and religiously principled state, and with the help of scientifically innovative Ajrawat Air-Pulse Autonomic Therapy, which promises a true homecoming for every individual who has been lost in a world of conditioned pain and material gain.

Chapter 7

A Daily Program for Healthy Living

In this final chapter, I describe the disciplines and habits you can develop in your daily life, to lead a healthy, pain free existence. Everything I describe below can be easily incorporated into your routine at home. Again, the cornerstone of healthy living is practicing Ajrawat Air-Pulse Autonomic Therapy on a daily basis. If you make it the centerpiece of the program described below, you will lead a life of physical health and emotional clarity and strength.

• Deconditioning of mind and disciplining the self

We must accept the fact that every one of us is the byproduct of various forms of conditioning, including cultural, religious, societal, political, and professional. One must also accept that to exist in a civilized world, one has to follow certain rules to be in harmony with oneself, society, and the environment, but at the same time without compromising one's own creativity, ingenuity, and free will. If one can learn early on to follow the route that lies between harmony with others and freedom for oneself, one truly can minimize a lot of the problems and stresses that inevitably arise in life.

Through Ajrawat Air-Pulse Autonomic Therapy, one can easily decondition one's mind and at the same time recondition it with self-determined affirmations, to feel mentally and physically healthy and self-empowered. While making those affirmations, one must not forget to follow the path of correct principles and righteousness. It is my true wish and hope that the practitioners of my scientific autonomic therapy will make this a better world for all.

One must always be aware of the foolish human need to control others through money, exploitation, sabotage, slander, and other treacherous means. One must be vigilant about these ego-based principles, which are detrimental to world harmony and peace. Each of us must make it our mission not to fall prey to these traps by staying honest, principled, and resolute in the fight by using our creativity, ingenuity, self-discipline, and determination. A true saint and soldier of conscience, who is homeostatically balanced and forward looking, will become self empowered and not trapped in a cycle of greed, power, and control.

• Daily religious prayer and affirmation—ethical and principled living characterized by honesty, equality, righteous social interaction, love, kindness, empathy, consideration, and one's choice of daily religious prayer

We live in a world where the majority of the population believes in one type of faith or another. Every religion has its own set of principles, based on philosophical conceptions or revelations. Some are more ecumenical while others are more judgmental. Those that are judgmental in nature have brought much misery and pain to this world through their condescension.

Wealth, cults and social status are mere manipulations to control other human beings through sophisticated and often condescending rituals and gestures. For a simple, less evolved mind, these manipulations become a holy gospel where one not only bows the head gently, but also bends the knee to another human being. People have been conditioned to do so out of sheer fear, resulting in a true loss of one's own autonomy that is passed down from one generation to the next, and the cycle of the human mind's inertia goes on unabated.

I fully respect every religion and its belief system, and wish their respective followers well. I believe that religious prayer is a philosophical tribute to our creator, and must be done daily with passion and sincerity and not as a mere ritual.

But when we look at the scientific evolution of all mankind, regardless of one's race, color, creed, origin, or religion, one reality invariably manifests the same for everyone—that is, the nervous system, neurotransmitters, and structures of the brain determine each person's intelligence, capabilities, emotions, and behaviors. One can truly create an optimal state of thinking, self-confidence, and self-esteem by balancing one's autonomic nervous system and by practicing correct principles. It is a state of mind one can create and maintain on one's own—a revolutionary concept that the world desperately needs to follow, and that can be aided by Ajrawat Air-Pulse Autonomic Meditation Therapy.

• Daily time for work, relaxation, family, or social events

In daily life there are a limited number of hours to sleep, work, eat, and to enjoy being with the family or friends. Human emotions and emotional intelligence must be nurtured and enhanced; otherwise, we become like helpless slaves, who become painfully compliant and complacent. Using your time well is essential for mental and physical balance. Work can be a great arena to use your skills and aptitudes to their fullest. But if work is only an endeavor to make ends meet, or becomes labor without love or a sense of accomplishment, it can become an ordeal affecting every system of the body in both subtle and profound ways.

If circumstances permit, one must make the time to be home with family, to allow time for discussion and communication, to play with children, engage in family recreation, and to participate in important social events. It is also important to allow twenty minutes in the morning and twenty minutes in the evening to meditate on yourself before starting and concluding your day. Ajrawat Air-Pulse Autonomic Therapy will help you live in the present, rather than in the past or future, which are conditioned states of mind and do not exist in reality.

• Daily reading: fiction, nonfiction, educational, or self-motivational

Daily reading is a great tool for mental stimulation. It improves brain function, especially cognition, and helps neurons grow. Combined with creative imagination, reading can make you strong and mentally powerful. In Albert Einstein's words, "Knowledge is power and imagination rules the world." Reading in all genres can boost your focus and self-confidence significantly.

Self-motivational and educational reading can take you further in your career and improve your social interaction with all members of society. It helps you become more self-reflective and introspective, and leads you closer to your ultimate goal of self-knowledge and realization. It helps you to truly gauge what has value in your life and to focus your time and energy on what is most important.

• Daily entertainment: TV, radio, music, or video games

A healthy balance must be maintained between intellectual stimulation from within and without. If you wish to put yourself in a trance and not be self aware, then TV or video games are a good option. If you wish to stay worldly and informed, then watching TV is surely an option and perhaps even a necessity. But you need to watch TV with discretion in order not become a pawn of the media's conditioning.

Music, such as symphonies, piano pieces, or easily played ethnic music, can help you generate alpha waves, which are soothing, relaxing, and can help lessen your anxiety and stress.

• Creativity, imagination, and ingenuity

The harsh and universal truth that all who are born must sooner or later die is one we must consciously acknowledge as soon as possible. Accepting this fact takes a lot of anxiety out of our daily existence. If we come to terms with the fact that we are here for only a brief period and that no glory lasts forever, it makes it all the more imperative to develop a mind that is free and sovereign, that can expand one's self-esteem, and that can experience the full bounty of life with imagination and creativity. Becoming a member of a fraternity or a secretive oath society can be very conducive and appealing to one's psyche, as it projects political power and control, but the flip side is that it negates your free and sovereign will—a big compromise towards becoming a star in your own galaxy or in the galaxies of the entire universe. In contrast, using your creative and imaginative freedom is far superior to living life with a conditioned mind, which follows the path created by someone else's doing and not one's own. Make it a point to explore your creativity, imagination, and ingenuity to the fullest, through a hobby, artistic pursuit, or other daily activity.

• Charity

"Sewa Kare So Chatar Hoye" ("Smart is the one who serves self-lessly.")

This is the philosophy I grew up with as a Sikh. Rendering service without the expectation of reward is one of the soundest principles of a life well lived. Freely giving to others without conditions takes you closer to the greater consciousness that brought you here. Actively participate in a charity or social endeavor of your choice. Sharing free food (Langar) with others creates a true sense of belonging with others—an endeavor which nurtures us emotionally, physically, and socially.

• Strengthening and stretching exercises, and alternating jogging with walking for physical conditioning and to build endurance and stamina (Dr. Ajrawat's Air-Pulse Marathon).

People who suffer from chronic pain usually have compromised physical functionality. They have often put on extra weight and have failed to condition their muscles, which once were active and easily maneuverable. This scenario is true for majority of human beings, who, while not suffering from chronic pain, have found their bodies compromised due to lack of exercise and conditioning. The body's muscles, lungs, and heart, which are vital to health, must be strength-ened on a regular basis, in order for our systems to function properly.

Without exercise and strengthening routines, muscles often lose their elasticity and strength, and the body as a whole is unable to per-form with power and agility. Lack of mobility can cause a person to visit the seventh stage of man, as described by William Shakespeare in his poem *Seven Ages of Man*, faster than one thought possible.

As I have discussed previously, myofascial pain is the most com-mon pain disorder and often results in secondary trauma of both a subtle and overt nature. Perpetuating factors, such as skeletal disproportion, can lead to the formation of trigger points in the muscles, which I have already discussed in detail. In order to be physically healthy and avoid myofascial pain, one must stretch and exercise daily.

So how does one maintain strength, balance, and agility throughout life?

Every patient of mine is directed to perform daily strengthening and stretching exercises to keep essential muscles healthy and intact, and to prevent the development of myofascial trigger points. Fifteen to twenty minutes of stretching daily (especially before exercise) will benefit the lower back, as well as the abdominal, hamstring, and quadriceps muscles. Stretching and exercising can make your day a lot easier physically, and therefore more productive.

One must remember that tight and aching muscles not only lead to pain and a limited range of motion, but can also make you tired and fatigued. Studies show that myofascial pain may be one of the major causes of depression. If complemented by sub-clinical hypothyroidism, it can sap all of your good energy and leave you totally fatigued.

In addition to performing strengthening exercises and stretching daily, also try alternating walking with jogging on a daily basis. For beginners, two to three minutes of walking alternated with two to three minutes of jogging is a good start, which can eventually be increased to three to five minutes at the most. Physiologically and anatomically, this is an optimal exercise, with minimal risk of stress and strain to the joints, back, heart, and other parts of the body. This exercise is based on my understanding that the body should be reconditioned or rehabilitated in a stepladder (or progressive) fashion, to restore lost functionality, muscle strength, range of motion, and physical agility.

When walking and jogging, keep in mind the golden rule that "slow and steady wins the race." Studies have shown that individuals who follow this regimen of alternating walking with jogging eventually do well in marathon running as well. Individuals who run marathons tend to live longer and lead more productive lives than those who live sedentary lives, watching marathons on TV.

• Self-preservation, self-defense, and martial arts training: Gatka, Krav Maga, Karate

We often feel very secure living in the United States, where the law of the land usually keeps everybody's personal security intact and safe. Thanks to our legal system and law enforcement, everybody's rights and safety are protected.

However, there are times when a situation can arise when your security or that of your family is threatened. This could happen to anyone in this country, but especially to a minority person who is confronted by someone who holds self-righteous views about racial or ethnic superiority. The threat could take the form of verbal assaults, but also could result in a physical attack.

As a Sikh, I was heartbroken to witness unprovoked attacks against Sikhs after the terrorist attacks of September 11, 2001. Although Sikhs had nothing to do with those events, they were physically assaulted and sometimes killed because they "looked" Middle Eastern (even though Sikhs do not come from that part of the world). My own son has encountered harassment and feared being attacked because he wears a turban and looks different than the average American. It was a very painful scenario to see innocent people singled out and blamed for a national tragedy for which they had no responsibility.

There may come a time when you may face an unprovoked physical threat from someone. If so, you must know how to protect yourself and your loved ones. The first and most lawful response is to call the police and register the case. But if that option isn't feasible, then one must be ready to use self-defense.

If so, what defense tools do you have at your disposal?

Gatka is an old Sikh martial art typically performed with a sword in the old days, when fending off an aggressor in that manner was not only acceptable but also highly effective. But in modern times, Gatka is used mostly for exhibition purposes.

Today, hand-to-hand fighting for defensive purposes tends to take the form of karate, judo, taekwondo, and others. But you can also send a warning signal to any potential attacker by adopting a certain posture and position. This can ward off an attack by an aggressor and save the situation for all parties. Violence must be avoided at all costs, but self defense and preservation of one's existence on righteous grounds must always be a top priority. To protect yourself, take up the study of a martial art of your choice. Krav Maga, a martial art for self-defense, has become very popular.

• Healthful and balanced diet

The entire world is becoming very conscientious about what we put into our systems daily. Food has become a huge issue, whether it's weight loss programs on the one hand and organic foods on the other. Regardless of how we regard food, the power of our taste buds to get us into bad eating habits remains profound. They can make us breach, many times over, our contract with ourselves to stay fit. In my experience psychology often yields to biology, whether it involves crème bulee or Ras Malai (both very tasty and extremely rich). This is a big problem.

Ajrawat Air-Pulse Autonomic Therapy helps people feel less depressed and therefore lose weight, as homeostatic balance gets restored in different parts of the brain and body. This minimizes one's desire to overeat, as hyperactivity in the taste buds is reduced. A balanced diet low in carbohydrates and high in proteins, fruits, and vegetables is the foundation of healthy nutrition.

Every culture has its own staple diet, and one can adjust one's diet preferences accordingly, so long as it's balanced. But I recommend following the balanced diet commonly used among Sikhs, which consists of the following foods:

Milk, buttermilk (lassi), tea, cornbread (makai-di-roti), tandoori roti (bread made in clay oven), spinach (saag), lentils (daal), beans (kidney, green), fresh vegetables like potatoes and cauliflower (alu-gobi), eggplant (bhartha), okra (bhindi), zuchini, salads (radishes, carrots, celery, scalions, lettuce, onions, cucumbers, ginger, green chili), use of cooking spices and condiments (garlic, cardamom, cloves, cinnamon, bay leaves, red and black pepper, mustard, and canola oil), long grain rice (basmati rice), chicken (curry or tandoori), goat or lamb curry, eggs, snacks like vegetable and paneer pakora (fritters), fried fresh water fish, desserts (kheer-rice pudding, ras malai, ladoo), and raw sugar (jagry or gur). In addition, I have started my own pioneering cuisine called Khalistani cuisine, which includes traditional and modern dishes based on good gastronomical principles. This new cuisine will be tasty, balanced, organic, and will cater to audiences worldwide.

Diabetics have their own particular needs, as do those who suffer from irritable bowel syndrome and lactose intolerance. Ajrawat Air-Pulse Autonomic Therapy, if done daily, will help you maintain a healthy gastrointestinal system.

• Vacation: change of scenario

Living in one habitat for a certain length of time can become monotonous, boring, stressful, and detrimental to one's daily living. Human beings need a change in routine. Taking a day off from work or a pre-planned vacation can be rejuvenating and refreshing for the brain and mental circuitry. A change of scene for even a few hours gives you a new focus visually and mentally. I take two vacations each year, between five to seven days each, which keeps me enthusiastic and determined in my work, my professional commitments, and my ongoing community service. I urge every reader to follow this regimen, if your circumstances permit.

• Practice the "Saint and The Soldier Concept"—learn to fight back against "The Tyrant," or the source of anxiety and depression.

The history of mankind is full of episodes where aggressors, tyrants, and barbarians massacred God-fearing and saintly people. The world watched, but refused to come to the rescue of those massacred. What options did the victims have? Turn the other cheek and be extinct, or stand up, confront, and fight the tyrant or oppressor. The latter option was definitely the best answer. Why?

If you stand up and fight, you further the cause of humanity. You make the statement that tyranny and evil shall not flourish and will not go unpunished. In our lives we will confront evil in both mental and physical forms, and we must fight against it. We must exist as both saints and soldiers, to make this a harmonious, healthy, and balanced world, where all have the right to exist and live peacefully.

We must always remember the famous statement by Martin Neimoller, speaking of the Nazis in Germany: "They came first for the Communists, and I didn't speak up because I wasn't a Communist. Then they came for the trade unionists, and I didn't speak up because I wasn't a trade unionist. Then they came for the Jews, and I didn't speak up because I wasn't a Jew. Then they came for me, and by that time no one was left to speak up."

The essential question remains this: why does any individual or group feel superior to others? Why do people have hate in their hearts for those who look different or who have a different belief system?

Again, it comes down to faulty conditioning, which is passed down from generation to generation. Though I have great reverence for established religions, the basic ethos of love, and the practice of correct principles, it is also time for every individual to realize his or her true potential by using more scientific and rational approaches. This can be done without losing respect for the philosophical ways in which religion preaches about God or the Greater Consciousness. I believe the time is right for us to enter this new frontier of spirituality, health, and actualization of self. As mind and body are not separate, in the same way science and religion are not separate. One uses equations while the other uses poetry, but both ultimately have the same logic and goal—knowing the creator. The time is ripe for us to explore a new frontier to achieve the same outcome, which we have tried through millennia via philosophical methods. If we embrace the scientific method or equation, we are bound to experience eternity. It is time for you to start your life fresh without the cobwebs of past conditioning, and yet with the opportunity to witness new horizons and walk on new paths leading through a new universe—a whole new paradigm   My sincere hope is that with the help of Ajrawat Air-Pulse Autonomic Therapy, we will be able to correct damaged circuitry and faulty states of mind, which in turn can help us all—both the oppressor and the oppressed.

Such an approach to living is what I hope you have learned from this book, and that you will now practice in your daily life.

Acknowledgements

The Autonomic Healing of Self, a book of solutions, is the result of my long-held dream to help humanity liberate itself from an endless cycle of mental and physical pain and stress. But without the help of numerous people, neither my pain management center nor the writing of this book would have been possible.

After being trained as a pain specialist, I encountered many limitations in my daily routine of treating pain and stress patients. For one, I was able to see only a limited number of patients daily, as each one needed my personal time and dedicated efforts to preserve the quality of care that I offer. Providing careful one-on-one attention to maintain a positive therapeutic alliance has been a sacrosanct principle of my medical care and the mission of my life. Without a caring and dedicated staff to help me, providing that kind of care would have been impossible.

My wife and staff psychiatrist, Dr. Sukhveen Kaur Ajrawat, through her dedication and commitment, has enabled me to provide kind and caring services to our pain and stress patients. Without her invaluable assistance, I could not possibly have achieved my professional goals as a pain specialist. Our patients not only appreciate our dedicated efforts towards their care, but also bless us with kind and complimentary words, which often make us feel as if we are their relatives. The warmth of our connection to our patients has been our greatest reward during the last 25 years.

When I introduced the new field of pain management to the Washington metropolitan area 25 years ago, I faced many challenges. I lacked experience in organizational matters, such as computers, billing, and dealing with insurance companies. It was my good luck to come across a kind and caring professional, whom I hired as my office manger. Ms. L. Carl has had the expertise and organizational skills to put my center on a firm footing, for which we will always be grateful. I also acknowledge my entire professional staff.

My wife and I have two boys, Sartaj Singh Ajrawat and Karan Singh Ajrawat, two bright and caring young men, who, besides my patients and my commitment to the political struggles of the Sikh community, have been the passion of my soul. One has decided to pursue a professional career in information technology, while the other wants to continue in the family tradition of medicine. They have been a great support for me in all my endeavors.

My older brother, Charanjit Singh Ajrawat, who was born with cerebral palsy, has always given me his unconditional love and counsel. I must also pay tribute to my mother and father, the late Dr. Pritam Singh and Mrs. Basant Kaur, who worked hard and helped me achieve my dream of becoming a physician, and my father-in-law, the late Col. Mukand Singh Sidhu and family, who was a very special, kind, and caring human being.

I must acknowledge my supporters in the Sikh community worldwide, who supported me over the last 32 years in my efforts to heal the wounds and pain they have suffered during their persecution by India. I also want to acknowledge Giani Kuldip Singh, Dr. Gurmit S. Aulakh, S. Simranjit S. Maan, the Late Col. Partap Singh, Rupinder S. Baath, Jaskaran S. Gill, G.S. Dhillon, Sukhdev S. Gill, I.S. Rekhi, M. Mohinder Singh, P.S. Giljian, Jagir Singh, Surjit S. Kalhar, Sukhdev Singh, Principal Sarwan Singh, the late Principal Dev Datt, the late Laszlo Dosa and Catherine Power Dosa, Dr. Navneet Singh, Dr. Anupam Mathur, Sartaj and Dr. Surinder S. Ajrawat, David S. Purewal, Pam and Major S. Purewal, J. S. Dhaliwal, Prof. Gurdarshan Singh Dhillon, and Bruce Marcus, Esq., who have been exceptional friends throughout my personal, community, and professional journey.

About the Author

Paramjit Singh Ajrawat, M.D., is Founder and Director of the Washington Pain Management Center. A fellowship trained pain specialist, certified in pain management/medicine, Dr. Ajrawat received his specialized training from a multidisciplinary pain management center at the University of Texas Health Center, San Antonio, Texas, where he was trained under various disciplines, including anesthesiology, physical medicine and rehabilitation, psychiatry, psychology, neurology, and orthopedic surgery.

Dr. Ajrawat received additional training in anesthesiology and critical care from Montefiore Hospital of the Albert Einstein College of Medicine of Yeshiva University in New York City. In addition, Dr. Ajrawat received two years of training in general and orthopedic surgery at the Erie County Medical Center of the State University of New York at Buffalo and at Brookdale Medical Center of Downstate University of New York, Brooklyn, New York.

Dr. Ajrawat introduced the field of pain management to the Washington metropolitan area in August 1985. He runs a full time interdisciplinary pain center along with his wife, Sukhveen Kaur Ajrawat, M.D., a board certified psychiatrist specializing in the psychiatric and psychological aspects of pain and stress.

Dr. Ajrawat is a member of various national and international pain organizations, including the International Association for the Study of Pain, the American Pain Society, the American Academy of Pain Management, and the American Academy of Pain Medicine.

He is founder of the International Association of Pain Specialists (IAPS) and the inventor of Dr. Ajrawat's Air-Pulse Meditation, Dr. Ajrawat's Air-Pulse Autonomic Meditation Therapy, Dr. Ajrawat's Air-Pulse Amygdala Therapy, and Dr. Ajrawat's Dynamic Model for Pain Management. He recently introduced a breakthrough treatment for diabetic neuropathy. Dr. Ajrawat is also the inventor of a patented (1994) head, neck, and shoulder exercise machine.

Dr. Ajrawat has written and published many articles on pain management in the local Washington area, as well as nationally and internationally. He has served as assistant clinical professor at Howard University School of Medicine, and has been a guest speaker on radio, TV, and at conferences worldwide. Dr. Ajrawat served as a special consultant to President George W. Bush on malpractice reform and presently serves as consultant on national health care reform. Currently Dr. Ajrawat serves as a consultant to several U.S. Senators and Congressmen on health care reforms.

As a Sikh community leader, Dr. Ajrawat spearheads the movement for reclamation of lost Sikh sovereignty and freedom, and for the establishment of a Sikh homeland in Punjab, Khalistan through peaceful, democratic, and political means. Dr. Ajrawat signed the covenant of Khalistan's admission into the UNPO General Assembly on Jan. 23, 1993 in Hague, The Netherlands. He is the founder and chief sponsor of the National Khalsa Day Parade, the Sikh community's national event, held each April in Washington, D.C.

Dr. Ajrawat is also a musician, singer, and plays multiple instruments, including guitar, harmonica, and djembe drums. His musical CD *Sovereignty of Sikhs* was recently released internationally and is available from *ITunes* and *Amazon.com*.

Notes

Notes

Notes

Notes

Notes

About the Washington Pain Management Center

Dr. Paramjit Singh Ajrawat founded the Washington Pain Management Center (WPM Center), a model self-supporting and independent pain center, in August 1985. The center is based on a specialist, interdisciplinary format, where a variety of services are offered under one roof to pain and stress sufferers.

Dr. Sukhveen Kaur Ajrawat, a board certified staff psychiatrist, is part of the center's interdisciplinary team. She was trained at Albert Einstein College of Medicine in New York City and received specialized training in the psychological and psychiatric aspects of pain and stress at the University of Texas Health Sciences Center in San Antonio, Texas. Dr. S. K. Ajrawat provides individual, family, and group psychotherapy at the center.

In addition, the Washington Pain Management Center employs consultants in every field of medicine, including neurology, orthopedic surgery, neurosurgery, oncology, medicine, surgery, radiology, and many others.

The pain management services at the center are based on the Bio-Psychosocial Model of illness and Dr. Ajrawat's Dynamic Model for treating and alleviating pain. This approach includes multimodality treatments addressing various components of chronic pain, including its physical, psychological, psychiatric, rehabilitative, social, and ergonomic aspects.

Professional, conservative, and quality care is provided to all patients on a one-to-one basis. Special emphasis is given to accurate and concrete diagnosis, a positive therapeutic alliance between physician and patient, careful follow-up treatments, and the patient's active participation at both the center and at home. Doctor shopping and use of polypharmacy is absolutely discouraged. Strict and stringent criteria are utilized to prevent unnecessary surgical interventions, drug dependency, and addiction.

Education of patients, the general public, and the medical community are an essential part of the center's mission. Clinical research on Ajrawat Air-Pulse Autonomic Therapy is ongoing at the WPM Center.

WPM Center is conveniently located in the Washington D.C. metropolitan area, near the beltway in Greenbelt, MD. For out of town and international patients, hotels are located within walking distance from the center. Select health care coverage, including Medicare, is accepted. Flexible payment schedules are offered to patients.

For more information or to schedule an appointment, contact:

The Washington Pain Management Center
Dr. Paramjit Singh Ajrawat, M.D.
7327A Hanover Parkway
Greenbelt, MD 20770
301.474.7246 or 1-800-783-PAIN (7246)
e-mail: psajrawat@gmail.com
web: PainManagement.com, PainSpecialist.com,
AutonomicHealingofSelf.com

P.S. Ajrawat, M.D.

About Dr. Ajrawat's
Air-Pulse Autonomic Meditation
Therapy Foundation

The goal of my charitable foundation is to help people suffering from pain and stress around the world. My foundation trains, certifies, and licenses individuals (volunteers) to administer and teach Ajrawat Air-Pulse Autonomic Meditation Therapy to medical students in medical school settings. These services can only be rendered on a voluntary basis without any monetary compensation. Only professionals who have passed a written exam, and who have been duly certified and licensed by the foundation, can teach Ajrawat Air-Pulse Autonomic Meditation Therapy. My foundation will also carry out essential research to further the cause of my groundbreaking and self-administered cognitive and medical therapy.

Ajrawat Air-Pulse Autonomic Meditation Therapy is copyrighted, federally registered, and patented. Dr. Paramjit Singh Ajrawat, M.D. and his foundation reserve all rights to teach and administer this therapy. The individual buying *The Autonomic Healing of Self* can learn how to practice autonomic therapy from the instructional DVD accompanying this book.

Dr. Ajrawat's Air-Pulse Autonomic
Meditation Therapy Foundation
P.O. Box 61505
Potomac, MD 20854, USA